CONGA DRUMMING

A BEGINNER'S GUIDE TO PLAYING WITH TIME

ALAN DWORSKY
AND BETSY SANSBY

DANCING HANDS MUSIC

Conga Drumming: A Beginner's Guide to Playing With Time

Published by Dancing Hands Music, 37 Thomas Ave. S., Suite 103, Minneapolis, MN 55405.

Printed in the United States of America by Viking Press.

Printed with soy ink on recycled, acid-free paper.

Five percent of all profits from the sale of this book go to the Rainforest Action Network.

cover art	Marie Olofsdotter, a visual artist in Minneapolis and author and illustrator of the award-winning picture book *Sofia and the Heartmender*.
inside illustrations	Jay Kendell, a freelance artist in Glendale, California.
book design	Anthony Desnick.
cover design	MacLean & Tuminelly in Minneapolis.
recording engineer	Jim Van Buskirk.

Library of Congress Catalog Card Number: 93 – 91079

Publisher's Cataloging in Publication

Dworsky, Alan L.
    Conga Drumming: a beginner's guide to playing with time / Alan Dworsky and Betsy Sansby.
        p. cm.
        Includes bibliographical references and index.
        ISBN 0-9638801-0-1

    1. Conga (Drum)–Methods–Self-instruction.
I. Sansby, Betsy. II. Title.

MT662.8.D96 1994   786.92'193
                        QBI93-22607

To Mickey Hart, whose book inspired us,
and to our wonderful teachers,
who taught us everything we know.

Special thanks to Tony Desnick, who always asked the right questions and encouraged us to search our souls for the answers; to Scott Sansby, who never thought we were crazy and whose original design work made this book seem real right from the start; to Linda Olson at Viking Press, who treated her littlest clients like big ones; to Nancy Tuminelly, whose generous guidance helped all along the way; to Jay Kendell, who figured out how to make hands dance; to Marie Olofsdotter, who brought our feelings to life in her art even when Isaac had ick; to Jim Van Buskirk, who always finds time to help an old friend; to everyone at LP Music Group for their continued support; and to Sandy Feldstein and Warner Bros. Publications.

Alan Dworsky spent 15 years as a professional keyboard player in rock, funk, and jazz bands. Then he went to law school. He is the author of *The Little Book on Legal Writing, The Little Book on Oral Argument,* and *User's Guide to the Bluebook.* He is now collaborating with Dean Magraw on an album combining percussion and guitar.

Betsy Sansby is a licensed marriage and family therapist and hypnotherapist in private practice.

Alan and Betsy are married and live with their daughter Molly in Minneapolis.

Contents

1

Welcome to the drum

The conga drum grabbed us a few years back and plunged us deep into the magical world of Afro-Cuban rhythms. It was as if after a lifetime of singing in unison we had suddenly discovered harmony. We found a way to meditate that didn't require silence, a source of community that didn't require words, and a wellspring of pleasure that never ran dry.

If your heart is beating, you're a drummer. Let the drum connect your heart to your hands. Let your hands learn to dance.

2

How this book works

This book will lead you step by step into a land of rhythmic enchantment. It teaches you how to play the conga drum using authentic Afro-Cuban rhythms: calypso, bomba, conga, rumba, bembe. While these rhythms are complex, the complexity often lies in the way different parts are interwoven rather than in the individual parts themselves. If you can keep steady time, there will always be some part that you can play. All the parts for each rhythm fit together like the pieces of an exquisite puzzle. This book presents the pieces one at a time and then shows you how to put them all together.

When we first started playing, we dug around in bookstores, libraries, and drum shops for a book containing these drum parts. We couldn't find one, probably because these rhythms haven't traditionally been written down. We did find general books on Latin percussion, but none focused specifically on the conga drum. So one by one–just for ourselves–we began to make and collect charts of the rhythms we were learning from our teachers. When we had assembled the drum parts for several popular rhythms, we decided to put this book together.

With the drum parts in written form, you should have an easier time learning them than we did. It's a challenge to correctly imitate a rhythm by simply watching a teacher play it, and an hour after a lesson, it's often hard to remember what you've learned. But chances are, if you can see a rhythm written on a page, you'll be able to pick it up faster and remember it more easily.

We use box charts to present the rhythms because they're easy for a beginner to understand and clearer than standard music notation for presenting most drum rhythms. We've also used symbols for the various hand strokes that are easy to memorize; each symbol suggests the sound or hand position of a particular stroke. Don't be intimidated by the unfamiliar look of the charts. The system of notation couldn't be simpler, and it's all explained in the next chapter.

We've also made our charts as big as possible because we got tired of squinting at small charts on the floor next to our drums. You'll be able to read them easily no matter how good your eyesight is and no matter where you put the book while you're playing. And you won't have to put your shoe on the book to hold it open because we've used a special binding that makes the book stay open and lie flat.

We haven't forgotten what it was like to be a beginner. It hasn't been all that long since we learned these rhythms ourselves. So besides writing them down, we've added comments that should make them easier for you to learn and hopefully will anticipate your questions. Sometimes we analyze the structure of the rhythms, sometimes we point out things you need to watch out for, and sometimes we use the rhythms to illustrate general principles of drumming.

The general principles are divided into three categories: Practice Principles, Playing Principles, and Group Playing Principles. Each principle is highlighted in the margin next to the text where it first appears. We've gathered these principles from many teachers and sources and have made explicit what are often unspoken rules of drumming.

The drum parts are arranged in order of difficulty, starting with the easiest and gradually progressing to the more challenging. For this reason, you'll find parts of the same rhythm presented in different chapters. We always tell you how to fit the parts together when it's time, and we often repeat the chart of a drum part so you don't have to search back through the book to find it.

The book is divided into lessons that contain roughly the amount of new material a teacher would present to you in a weekly lesson. But how much time you spend on each lesson is entirely up to you. Go at your own pace. Take as much time as you need to make each rhythm come alive in your hands.

You don't need any experience with drumming to understand this book. In fact, we explain the rhythms as if you had no musical experience at all. When a traditional musical term or concept can't be avoided, it's set apart from the text and explained in a specially-marked box called a Musical Time-Out.

If you do have experience drumming, you'll still find plenty here that's new and challenging. Although the book starts with the basics, the advanced rhythms require considerable skill, and the later chapters should be a stretch even for advanced players.

**Take as much time as you need
to make each rhythm come alive in your hands.**

A single conga drum is the only thing you need to play these rhythms. Most of them are meant to be played on a single drum, and those that are meant for two can be adapted for one.

If you don't have a conga drum and can't afford one right now, you can still learn the rhythms. We've played for hours on kitchen pots, upside down wastebaskets, and Quaker Oats boxes, so we know that you can make a lot of progress without the ideal instrument. But to really produce the sounds of the rhythms, at some point you're going to want to get a conga drum. Or two.

The book is designed so you can learn conga drumming all by yourself. The rhythms sound great and are satisfying for one person to play alone. But they are also parts of larger rhythms played by many drums and percussion instruments. When you know the conga drum parts in this book, you'll know how to join in when you find a group playing the rhythms. Ideally, however, you should try to find or create a group to play with right from the start, so you can learn the drum parts in their full rhythmic context.

If you can't find a group, find a partner to play with. You'll learn twice as fast and have twice as much fun. Just knowing that your partner is counting on you will help you keep to a regular practice schedule. When you play different parts at the same time, you'll hear how rhythms fit together and learn to listen while you play. And when you get stuck, you'll have someone there to pull you out; when the rhythms are flowing, you'll have someone there to celebrate with.

The recording that comes with this book includes each of the 175 individual drum parts covered in the book as well as the complete rhythms played with all the parts. Use the recording as you work through the book to help you learn each individual part and to hear how all the parts fit together. It's especially helpful if you don't have a partner or group to play with.

You'll deepen your appreciation of the rhythms in this book by learning about their history and the context in which they are played. Afro-Cuban rhythms have their roots in African rhythms brought across the Atlantic by slaves. They acquired their distinctive style in Cuba and other Caribbean countries, where they continue to be an integral part of the songs, dances, and ceremonies that define community life. They also evolved in the music of dance bands that have made them popular around the world in the style now commonly called salsa. In the back of the book we refer you to sources for further study. Our hope is that by giving you help in learning to play the conga drum, you'll be inspired to go beyond this book and seek out teachers who can give you what we cannot.

The orchid is an exotic tropical flower native to the Caribbean. To experience an orchid in its native soil, surrounded by the sights, sounds, and smells of a tropical rainforest, is to experience it in its fullness. But all over this country, from the tiny apartment in New York City to the backyard terrace in San Francisco, people are bringing beauty into their lives by growing orchids, and all over this country people are gathering together to play Afro-Cuban rhythms. These rhythms have a vitality that transcends context. All you need to do to feel that force is to play them.

3

A simple system of notation

Here's what the box charts in this book look like:

1	+	2	+	3	+	4	+
△			○		○	○	
R			L		L	R	

They may look complicated at first, but they're really very simple and are by far the easiest drum charts to read.

Each vertical row of boxes shows what's happening on a single beat. Each horizontal row gives you a different kind of information. The top row tells you how to count the rhythm. The next row tells you when and how to hit the drum. If there's a symbol in a box, you hit the drum on that beat in the way indicated by the symbol. For example, in the chart above, in the box under beat 1, there's a triangle. The triangle is the symbol for the slap, so you play a slap on beat 1. If a box is empty, like the box under beat 2, you play nothing on that beat.

Here are all the symbols for how to hit the drum:

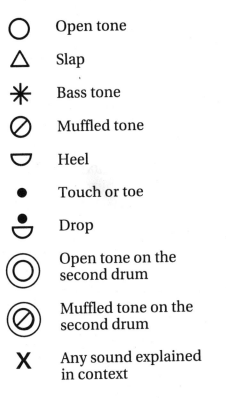

◯	Open tone
△	Slap
✳	Bass tone
⊘	Muffled tone
▽	Heel
●	Touch or toe
⊖	Drop
◎	Open tone on the second drum
⊘	Muffled tone on the second drum
X	Any sound explained in context

The bottom row of the chart tells you which hand to use. You'll be using both hands in all the rhythms, but the right hand often plays a dominant role. If you're left-handed, you can reverse the hands.

Sometimes charts will include other rows, such as a row indicating something you're supposed to say or sing. And about halfway through the book we start charting clave and cowbell parts by circling numbers on the count row. But you don't need to worry about these now; we'll explain them when you need them.

To make the charts as big as possible, we've made most of them just long enough to show a single repetition of each rhythm. But regardless of the length of the chart, you should always play each rhythm over and over. When you get to the end of a chart, go back to the beginning as if the rhythm were written in a circle, and don't stop between repetitions.

This system of notation works great for teaching you the basic structures of the rhythms in this book. The recording that comes with the book will also help. But to really get a feel for how the rhythms are performed, there's no substitute for hearing the real thing. So listen to as much recorded Afro-Cuban music as possible, and watch for live performances in your area.

After listening to a few performances, you'll be able to pick out the basic rhythms you're learning here, but you'll notice that they are played in a variety of ways. There is no one correct version of any of these rhythms. Which instruments are used often depends on something as mundane as who shows up to play and what they bring with them. In rural areas of the Caribbean, the rhythms are played in a traditional style known as "folkloric," while in the city, nightclub bands play a more eclectic style, blending traditional rhythms with elements of North American jazz, funk, and rock. Every teacher will teach a slightly different version of these rhythms. When you play with other drummers, you'll hear these differences. Don't worry. If you learn to play the rhythms as they are presented in this book, you'll be able to adjust easily and play with confidence.

4

Learning to hit the drum using rhythms in four

You've probably come to the drum with a hunger for its rhythms and limited patience for technical discussion. We try to satisfy that hunger by giving you authentic rhythms to play right from the start. But we'd be doing you a disservice if we gave you only what you want instead of what we know you need.

Proper technique is critical. You need it to protect your hands, which can be easily bruised by hitting the drum improperly. You also need it to create the contrasts and textures that give the conga drum its distinct sound: your slaps must be sharp, your open tones round, your bass tones thick. Good technique distinguishes tasty conga drumming from ordinary beat borscht.

There are many different styles of conga drumming. Techniques vary widely from place to place and from individual to individual. The techniques in this book reflect the way we were taught to play the drum, and are standard in the Afro-Cuban style of playing. Experienced drummers might differ on some of the details, but most would agree on the fundamentals. Take what we have to offer, combine it with what you learn from others, and–always–consult your own body. Find what works for you.

Good technique distinguishes tasty conga drumming from ordinary beat borscht.

Introductory lesson

Choosing the right drum

Each drum has its own voice, so it's important to find one that speaks to you. But until your ear becomes attuned to the language of drums, it can be hard to tell one from another. If you're a beginner, bring an experienced player with you when you go looking for a drum. Having someone who can produce the full range of sounds on the drum will help you make a more informed decision. Here are a few other things to consider.

Material
Conga drums are made from fiberglass or wood, and you can find a great drum made out of either material. Fiberglass drums tend to be louder and more durable; wooden drums tend to have a sweeter, mellower sound and be more sensitive to changes in temperature and humidity.

Weight
Drums vary a lot in weight, so if you find one you like, pick it up to see how heavy it is. If you plan to play in one place, weight won't matter much. But if you're going to be carrying it up and down stairs or lifting it in and out of your car a lot, weight can make a big difference.

Height
Drums vary in height from about 28 inches to 32 inches. Most are about 30 inches, which is a good size for someone about 5 foot 9 inches tall or more sitting on an ordinary chair. If you're shorter than 5 foot 9, you'll probably need to sit higher to play a 30 inch drum comfortably. If you're shorter than 5 foot 4, you may want to consider getting a shorter drum.

Diameter
Conga drums are grouped by size into three categories. The diameter of the head determines which category a drum is in. The tumba (TOOM-bah) is the largest and has the lowest pitch; it's head is usually about 12 1/2 inches across or more. The quinto (KEEN-toh) is the smallest and has the highest pitch; it's head is usually about 11 inches across or less. The

conga (CONE-gah) falls in the middle. If you're buying your first drum, to give yourself maximum flexibility get the middle-sized drum: the conga.

Location of metal ring
The skin across the head of a drum is held on with a metal ring. When the ring is almost level with the drumhead, it's easy to bruise your hands on it unless you're very careful about technique. We recommend that you find a drum that has a metal ring a couple inches below the level of the head.

Method of tuning
Most conga drums are tuned by tightening or loosening metal lugs that hold the head in place. African conga drums– called ashikos–are tuned by tightening or loosening ropes that hold the head in place. Drums with metal lugs are quicker and easier to tune, but some drummers prefer an ashiko because they like a drum without hardware and enjoy the more strenuous ritual of tuning with ropes.

Age
A good drum that's properly cared for can last a lifetime. Drumheads do lose their resiliency after a while, and sometimes replacing a head will bring an old drum back to life. If you're looking at used drums, check to be sure that the body isn't cracked and that the head is still round and not warped from overtightening.

How to tune a drum

Before you play your drum, you may need to tune it. The head should be fairly tight and produce a tone that sounds good to you. If your drum has metal lugs and you want the tone to be higher, go around the drum tightening each lug in order, a little bit at a time. If you want the tone lower, loosen each lug the same way. Adjusting the lugs equally and gradually will ensure that there's even pressure on the head, so the drum doesn't get pulled out of shape. To test whether the lugs are tightened evenly, go around the head making a tone near each lug; all the tones should be the same pitch.

If you have trouble remembering which way to turn the lugs at first, and find yourself down on the floor looking up to figure out which way is clockwise, there's an easier way: Tight to the right and loose to the left. As you look down at your hand holding the wrench, tighten a lug by moving the handle to the right; loosen it by moving the handle to the left.

The instructions that came with our drums said that we should loosen the lugs completely whenever we're not playing to preserve the head, but we've never done that and we don't know anyone who has. We like the head to be tight all the time so we can grab the drum and start playing whenever we feel like it.

Playing position

Most experienced drummers play sitting down with the drum resting directly on the floor. When you're sitting, you're stable, and that makes your playing more precise. You also have more control over the sound of the drum, because you can change its tone by tilting it at different angles. And if you're playing for more than an hour, sitting is generally the most comfortable position.

Playing Principle
Play sitting down for greatest stability, control, and comfort.

You can play standing if it's more comfortable, or alternate between sitting and standing. It's up to you. If you do play standing, the drum should rest on a stand that lifts it off the floor and puts the drumhead at about the same height in relation to your body as when you were sitting. This also makes the drum louder, but it limits your control of the sound. You have greater freedom of movement when you stand, but your hands are less stable. When you see a conga drummer in a band play standing up, it's often for show or to make the drums louder, not because it's better to play that way.

Playing Principle
Tilt the drum forward or to the side to let the sound out the bottom.

So now that you've decided to play sitting down, find a chair that's the right height and that doesn't have arms you can bump your elbows on. Sit on the edge of the chair with your back straight and put the drum between your legs like the drummers on the cover of this book. Relax your shoulders and put your hands on the drumhead. If your forearms aren't roughly parallel to the floor, adjust the height at which you're sitting until they are.

Tilt the drum forward or to the side to let the sound come out the bottom. Find the angle at which the drum almost balances by itself on its edge while tilted. Then gently steady it with your thighs; don't grip it between them. You can also use your feet or ankles to steady the drum at the bottom. If the floor is carpeted, you can put a flat piece of wood under the drum so the sound doesn't get absorbed by the carpet.

Playing Principle
Gently steady the drum with your thighs and ankles; don't grip it.

Before you start playing, you need to make sure nothing is going to hit the drum but your hands. So roll up your sleeves if they have buttons that might clack or scrape against the drum. Take off any bracelets that might do the same. And be sure to take off any rings; they can hurt the drum and your hands. We don't even bother putting our wedding rings on anymore. We were constantly having to take them off to play and then regularly forgetting where we put them. Now they're safe together in a drawer.

Take off your watch too, even if it isn't in the way. Don't saddle your hands with a mechanical chaperon. It's time to play.

Lesson 1

Calypso high and middle drum parts and the open tone and touch

Many techniques give conga drumming its distinctive sound, but the two that stand out the most are open tones and slaps. We start with open tones because they're easy to play and because they're often perceived as the essence of a rhythm. They stand out because the tone is the only sound on the drum that has a definite and clear pitch. When several drummers play different parts of a rhythm together, you'll hear a melody by listening to the open tones.

To make the open tone, you first need to know where to put your hands. Think of the drumhead as the face of an old-fashioned clock. Point your hands towards the center. On a middle-sized drum, your right hand should be between the 4 and 5 and your left hand between the 7 and 8. Keep your hands in line with your forearms, so that you could draw a straight line from your elbow through your middle finger. Consider this hand position as home base. Most of the strokes are played from this position:

The open tone is made by bouncing your fingers off the drumhead. You'll get the correct bounce and make the right sound by focusing not on the fingers but rather on the relation of your palm to the edge of the drum. If you get your palm in the right position, the fingers will take care of themselves.

Start with either hand a couple inches above the drum. Bring your hand to the drum by simply lowering it with the forearm and adding a little wrist action. Your palm should hit the edge of the drumhead just below the joints where the fingers attach to the palm–hitting directly on the joints will injure them:

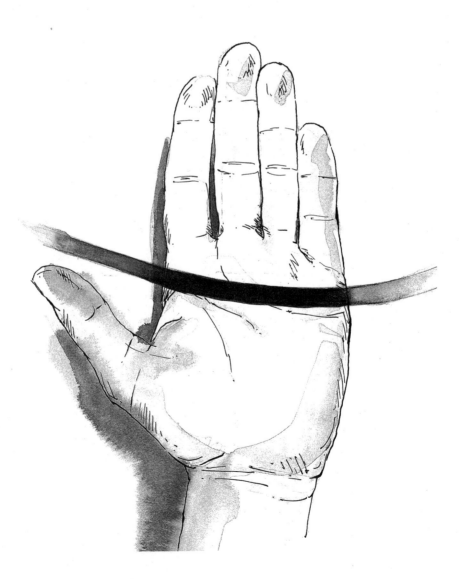

Memory tip
*The circle is round and
the open tone has a round
sound.*

Keep your fingers together, but keep the thumb out of the
way by pulling it either up or back so you don't whack it on
the edge of the drum. When the palm hits the edge of the
drum, your hand should be in line with your forearm and
your hand and forearm together should be pointed up at a
slight angle:

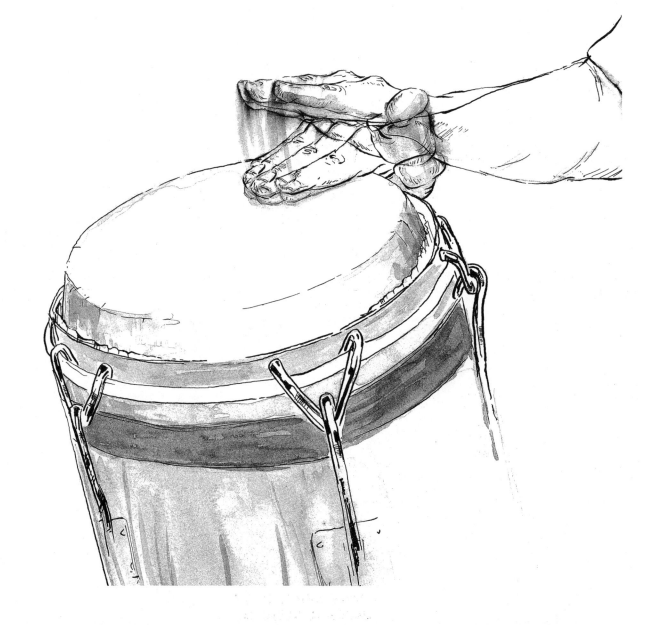

Keep your fingers relaxed, so that when the palm hits the edge of the drum, the fingers automatically bounce down and back up. When they finish the bounce, they should be back in line with the hand and forearm. After finishing the stroke, you can either leave the palm resting on the edge of the drum or lift the hand immediately to make the next stroke.

A good open tone should have a clear, round sound with a distinct pitch. To contribute to the melody when you play in a group, your open tones must sing.

Group Playing Principle
Make your open tones sing.

Now you're ready to play your first authentic rhythm. It's the high drum part from calypso, a rhythm that originated in Trinidad. It's nothing flashy by itself, but when you hear it played along with the other parts in calypso, you'll appreciate how important it is.

Musical Time-Out: Beats in four

A beat is a unit of musical time and a measure is a group of beats. Most of the rhythms in this book are charted in 4/4 time, which we call "four" for short. In 4/4 time, measures are divided into 4 numbered beats. If each of the 4 numbered beats were undivided, each would be a quarter note, and each would take up one quarter of the length of the measure:

1	2	3	4

When you divide each of the 4 quarter notes in half you get 8 eighth notes. In all the charts in four in this book, the 4 quarter notes in a measure are divided into 8 eighth notes, and each box in a chart stands for one of those eighth notes:

1	+	2	+	3	+	4	+

The symbol "+" is read as "AND."

Practice principal
Count out loud while you play each new rhythm.

To play your first rhythm, all you need to do is alternate hands playing open tones on the correct beats. At first, count out loud while you play: "1 AND 2 AND 3 AND 4 AND." Try to make all the tones sound the same:

Rhythm 1-1: Calypso high drum part

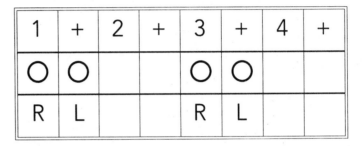

1	+	2	+	3	+	4	+
O	O			O	O		
R	L			R	L		

Repeat this rhythm–and all the other rhythms in this book–over and over without any break. Imagine that the chart is written in a circle, so that 1 follows immediately after the AND of 4.

You can hear how this rhythm sounds on the recording that comes with this book. All the numbered rhythms in the book are presented in order on the recording. Whenever we tell you to combine rhythms, you can hear the rhythms combined at the corresponding spot on the recording.

Now you're ready for the next stroke: the touch. It's the easiest stroke to make and the quietest. All you do is touch the drumhead lightly with the pads of your fingertips. Start with your hands at home base: in the same position as for the open tone. Then, alternating hands, simply drop your fingertips to the drumhead and raise them. Your palms do not make contact with the drum:

●

Memory tip
The dot is the smallest symbol and the touch makes the smallest sound.

The touch serves mainly as a timekeeper between louder strokes, helping your hands to flow and adding a subtle fullness to a rhythm. You're free to add timekeeping touches–sometimes called ghosts or ghost strokes–in any rhythm. But you must keep them light enough so they don't change the basic sound of the rhythm you're playing.

Now that you know two strokes, you're ready to put them together and play a second rhythm. It's the middle drum part from calypso. At first, count out loud while you play:

Playing Principle
To add fullness or flow to a rhythm, play touches where there are no notes.

Rhythm 1-2: Calypso middle drum part

1	+	2	+	3	+	4	+
◯	●	●	◯	◯	●	●	●
R	L	R	L	R	L	R	L

Play this rhythm–and every new rhythm–slowly at first. Strive for accuracy over speed, control over power. Speed and power will come naturally over time.

Now that you have two drum parts to calypso, you've got your first opportunity to play a duet with someone. If you don't yet have someone to play with, you can hear how the two parts fit together on the recording.

Practice Principle
Play every new rhythm slowly at first.

**Strive for accuracy over speed,
control over power.**

Lesson 2

Conga high drum part and the slap

In this lesson you're going to learn the technique that stands out in dramatic contrast to the open tone: the slap. The slap has a sharp sound like the crack of a whip, just the opposite of the round sound of the open tone.

Although the slap looks simple, it's often challenging to learn and it takes practice to master. Be patient with yourself. It always comes with time.

The slap is made by bringing the pads of your fingertips down in a whip-like motion onto the drumhead. As with the open tone, the relation of your palm to the edge of the drum is critical. When you make the slap, your hand hits the edge of the drum on the bottom half of the palm, instead of the upper half as it does for the open tone. So when you go from an open tone to a slap, your hand will shift slightly toward the center of the drum.

To make the slap, start from the same position that you started from to make the open tone. Pivot your hand upward from the wrist. Then whip your fingers down onto the drumhead while driving your palm down and slightly forward onto the edge of the drum. Cup your hand so that only the pads of the fingertips hit the head. The cup should be slight; you should only be able to slide a pencil between your palm and the drumhead, not a golf ball.

Keep your fingers together or slightly apart, and keep the thumb out of the way as you did with the open tone. After making the slap, leave your fingertips on the drumhead for a moment and don't let them bounce up immediately. It may help at first to slightly grip the head. Leaving your fingertips on the head prevents it from vibrating and helps give the slap a crisp sound:

△

Memory Tip
The triangle has sharp points and slaps have a sharp sound.

When you leave your fingertips on the drum for a moment after making a slap–as in this lesson–the stroke is called a closed slap. When you let your fingertips bounce off the head immediately, the stroke is called an open slap. The open slap usually takes even longer to master than the closed slap, and isn't necessary for playing the rhythms in this book. Once you've mastered closed slaps, if you play them fast enough they'll naturally turn into open slaps because you won't have time to keep your fingertips on the drum.

The sound of the slap does not come from sheer force but rather from the snap of the wrist. Think of the hand as a whip. It doesn't take much force at the handle to make the tip crack. The main thing to remember is to keep your hand relaxed.

Now you're ready to try out your slaps by playing the high drum part from the rhythm called conga (CONE-gah). Start out playing slowly and counting out loud:

Rhythm 2-1: Conga high drum part

1	+	2	+	3	+	4	+
		△	△			O	O
		R	L			R	L

Playing Principle
Muffling the head with one hand while playing a slap with the other makes the slap sound crisper.

Playing Principle
Whenever you play an open tone in one hand, the other hand must be completely off the head so the open tone won't be muffled.

Whenever it's convenient, you can make a slap sound even crisper by muffling the head with one hand while playing the slap with the other. You'll hear the difference right away. In this rhythm, it's easy to do this by leaving the right hand on the head until after you've played the slap in the left. You don't have to press down hard with the muffling hand; just let it rest on the head.

Whenever you play an open tone, however, the hand that's not playing the stroke must be completely off the head or the tone will be muffled. So in this rhythm, be sure the fingers of your left hand aren't still on the head when your right hand plays the open tone on 4.

Now you're going to play the same rhythm in slightly different form. You're going to add touches where there are no notes to fill out the sound of the rhythm and help you keep time:

Rhythm 2-2: Conga high drum part

1	+	2	+	3	+	4	+
●	●	△	△	●	●	◯	◯
R	L	R	L	R	L	R	L

A final word of warning: Of all the strokes, the slap is probably the hardest on your hands. If you see drummers with tape on their fingers, it's often to cover bruises or callouses they've developed from playing slaps too hard. So be careful with slaps, especially when you're just learning how to play them. Protect your hands by using proper technique. As time goes on, you'll be playing sharp slaps with less and less force and movement.

Use common sense to protect your hands. If you're playing long, play light. If you're playing in a group, don't fight to be heard over the other drummers. Don't even worry about hearing yourself. Concentrate on the feel of what you're playing and focus on the sound of the group.

If your hands do start to hurt, stop playing until they stop hurting. Before you start playing again, take the time to analyze the problem. If you continue to play on an injured hand, you may do permanent damage. You've got a long drumming career ahead of you; don't jeopardize it by playing in pain.

Playing Principle
If your hands start to hurt, stop playing and don't start again until they've healed and you've analyzed the problem.

Lesson 3

Rumba low drum part and the bass tone

The visceral thud of a bass tone is often more felt than heard. The rich sound resonates in the chest like an amplified heartbeat. Driving your full palm into the drum can feel like sinking it deep into the earth. When you lift your hand after playing a good bass tone, don't be surprised if it's covered with mud.

To understand how to make the bass tone, think of your palm as an airplane coming in for a landing. Starting with either hand a couple inches above the drumhead, bring the palm down and slightly forward, not straight down. To add oomph, flick your wrist slightly to drive the palm into the head. Without tensing your fingers, hold them up just high enough so they don't hit the head.

Your right palm should land to the right of the center of the drumhead and your left palm to the left. Don't extend your hands any further forward than necessary; the palms only need to land about an inch or two from the edge of the drum. This maximizes your speed and efficiency, which you'll appreciate when you try to play fast or play for a long time.

**Driving your full palm into the drum
can be like sinking it deep into the earth;
when you lift your hand, don't be surprised
if it's covered with mud.**

✳
Memory Tip
The asterisk is a like a big inkblot spread out on the page; on a bass tone your palm is spread out on the drumhead.

Playing Principle
When you alternate playing bass tones in both hands, point your hands almost straight ahead.

When you alternate playing bass tones in both hands, to fit them on the head and avoid collisions you have to point them almost straight ahead. This means your wrists will be slightly bent and you won't be able to draw a straight line from your forearm through your middle finger:

Now you're ready to learn a rhythm with bass tones. It's a low drum part in the rhythm called rumba (ROOM-bah). Rumba is not only the name of a rhythm, but also the name for a gathering involving music, dance, and celebration. There are several styles of rumba, including yambu, columbia, and guaguanco (wah-wahn-KOH). In this book you'll be learning the style called rumba guaguanco.

The rumba low drum part combines two bass tones with an open tone. Count out loud while you play until you're sure you've got it:

Rhythm 3-1: Rumba low drum part

1	+	2	+	3	+	4	+
✳				✳		O	
L				L		R	

Remember to lift the left hand off the drumhead before you play the open tone in the right hand, or the tone will be muffled.

By now, you should already be on your way to developing some good practice rituals. Notice what works for you. Tuning in to your own internal rhythms will help you find the time of day when your hands feel best and your concentration is at its peak. And you may find a particular place to play where you feel most comfortable and least inhibited.

Practice Principle
Develop practice rituals that work for you.

Once you've found your time and place, try to establish a regular practice schedule; it's better to practice five minutes a day than an hour once a week. Whenever you have a long practice session, take breaks to stretch and refresh yourself. Quit while you still have energy and end on a high note.

Practice Principle
Practice regularly; it's better to practice five minutes a day than an hour once a week.

Lesson 4

Tumbao and the heel and toe

Think of the hand as a foot. The heel is the base of the palm; the toes are the fingertips. The heel stroke is made by lowering the wrist and dropping the base of your palm to the drumhead, while keeping the rest of your hand and your fingers up:

The heel stroke is like a bass stroke except that you hit the drumhead with less of your palm. Your heel should hit the drumhead an inch or two from the edge of the drum, just as it does on a bass stroke.

The toe stroke is just a touch that goes with a heel stroke. Since the strokes are the same, we use the same symbol for both the toe and the touch. Like the touch, the toe stroke is light; just let your fingertips fall to the drumhead.

When one hand alternates playing heels and toes, it rocks back and forth like a seesaw. When the heel goes down, the fingers come up; when the fingers go down, the heel comes up.

By alternating hands playing a heel-toe stroke, you can get a fast roll going. Start this next rhythm slowly and then gradually build speed until you're playing it as fast as you can:

●
Memory Tip
*Since the toe and the touch
are the same stroke, the
symbol is the same for both .*

Rhythm 4-1: Heel-toe pattern

1	+	2	+	3	+	4	+
⏝	●	⏝	●	⏝	●	⏝	●
R	R	L	L	R	R	L	L

When you really get going on this one, the rocking motion will become less pronounced. Neither the heel nor toe will remain in contact with the drumhead for more than an instant. Your hand will just drop, flutter on the head, and then rise again. The pattern played evenly at high speed will sound like the purring of a cat.

Now you're ready for one of the most popular and versatile conga drum rhythms: tumbao (TOOM-bow). It's the main conga part used in much of contemporary Afro-Cuban music. It also fits well with rock, funk, and jazz, so expect to be playing it a lot. Before enlightenment, play tumbao. After enlightenment, play tumbao.

Playing Principle *Whenever one hand plays up on the drumhead and the other at the edge of the drum, the hands should form a "T."*

Tumbao has a heel-toe pattern in the left hand, with slaps and tones in the right. Whenever one hand plays up on the drumhead and the other at the edge of the drum, the hands should form a "T":

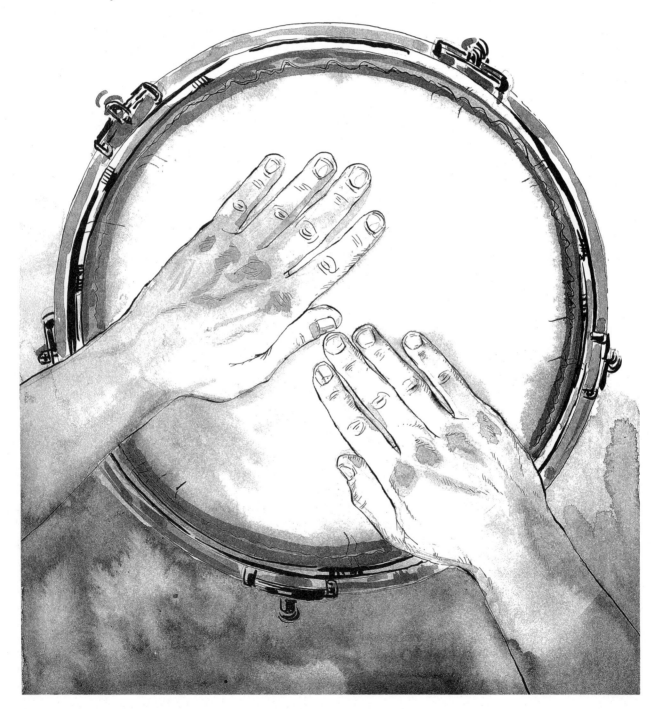

This is the position your hands should be in when you play tumbao.

The first version of tumbao here has two slaps. After you play the first heel in the left hand, leave your palm on the head while dropping the fingers to make the toe stroke. Your left hand will then be resting on the head as you play the slaps in the right hand. Play the second heel-toe like the first, but after finishing the toe stroke lift the left hand completely off the drum before playing the open tones in the right hand:

Rhythm 4-2: Two-slap tumbao

1	+	2	+	3	+	4	+
⌣	•	△	△	⌣	•	○	○
L	L	R	R	L	L	R	R

Notice the similarity between the sound of this rhythm and the sound of the conga high drum part you learned in Lesson 2.

The next version of tumbao could probably be called the standard version. It has only one slap in the right hand. The left hand does something new–starting on the AND of 2, it begins rocking on the toe instead of the heel:

Rhythm 4-3: Tumbao

1	+	2	+	3	+	4	+
⌣	•	△	•	⌣	•	○	○
L	L	R	L	L	L	R	R

Because tumbao fits with so many rhythms, it's great for practicing with recorded music. When you're a beginner,

Practice Principle
Play along with recorded music.

playing along with recorded music is often the only way to get the feel of playing with a full band. It's also a great way to learn to listen to other parts while holding your own. Since we got our CD player, we've had the privilege of playing tumbao with Tito Puente, Lee Ritenour, Youssou N'Dour, and Giovanni Hidalgo–and not one of them has complained about our playing.

Lesson 5

Calypso middle drum part extended

You're not going to learn any new techniques in this lesson. Instead you're going to learn the second half of the calypso middle drum part you learned in Lesson 1. When combined, the two halves form a single two-measure phrase.

The second half is more challenging than the first because the phrase made by the open tones does not begin on 1. The first open tone is on the AND of 1:

Rhythm 5-1: Calypso middle drum part (2nd half)

1	+	2	+	3	+	4	+
●	O	●	O	O	O	●	●
R	L	R	L	R	L	R	L

Here are the two halves combined. The full rhythm takes two measures and the measures are separated by a dark vertical line:

Rhythm 5-2: Calypso middle drum part

1	+	2	+	3	+	4	+	1	+	2	+	3	+	4	+
O	●	●	O	O	●	●	●	●	O	●	O	O	O	●	●
R	L	R	L	R	L	R	L	R	L	R	L	R	L	R	L

If you find yourself stumbling when you try to play this rhythm fast, stop. Go back to playing it slow. If one part of the rhythm is tripping you up, isolate it and practice it separately. If you're still having trouble, put your hands in your lap, close your eyes and visualize yourself playing the rhythm correctly. Or take your drum into a different room; a change of scenery sometimes helps. If nothing works, take a break and practice something else, and come back to the rhythm when you're fresh.

Practice Principle
Isolate difficult parts of a rhythm and practice them separately.

Whatever you do, don't grind in mistakes. Playing a rhythm incorrectly over and over only teaches your hands to play it incorrectly. Don't beat yourself up. Everybody makes mistakes. The key is knowing how to avoid repeating them.

Practice Principle
Don't grind in mistakes.

Lesson 6

Bomba low drum part

In this lesson, you're going to use the techniques you already know and learn a new rhythm. It's the low drum part from bomba (BOHM-bah), a rhythm that originated in Puerto Rico.

We've broken the low drum part in half so you can learn it more easily. Here's the first half:

Rhythm 6-1: Bomba low drum part (1st half)

1	+	2	+	3	+	4	+
△			○		○	○	
R			L		L	R	

This drum part can also be played with a different hand pattern:

Rhythm 6-2: Bomba low drum part (1st half)

1	+	2	+	3	+	4	+
△			O		O	O	
R			L		R	L	

Notice the difference between these two hand patterns. In the first version, the right hand plays on the on-beats: 1 and 4. The left hand plays on the off-beats: the ANDs of 2 and 3. Some drummers arrange their hand patterns so that they play on-beats in the right hand and off-beats in the left as much as possible. Playing this way makes it easy to keep track of where you are in a rhythm.

Musical Time-Out: On-beats and off-beats

When we refer to "on-beats" in four we mean the numbered beats 1, 2, 3, and 4. When we refer to "off-beats" we mean the ANDs of each of the numbered beats. Some theorists dispute whether there really are on-beats and off-beats in Afro-Cuban music, but we find these concepts to be useful in analyzing the rhythms.

Playing Principle
It doesn't matter what hand pattern you use as long as the rhythm sounds good.

Other drummers arrange their hand patterns to alternate hands as much as possible. Those drummers would prefer the second version. It doesn't matter what hand pattern you use as long as a rhythm sounds good.

The second half of the low drum part is identical to the first except that it has four open tones instead of three. Here it is, using the first hand pattern above:

Rhythm 6-3: Bomba low drum part (2nd half)

1	+	2	+	3	+	4	+
△			O	O	O	O	
R			L	R	L	R	

Now put the two halves together and play them as one rhythm:

Rhythm 6-4: Bomba low drum part

1	+	2	+	3	+	4	+	1	+	2	+	3	+	4	+
△			O		O	O		△			O	O	O	O	
R			L		L	R		R			L	R	L	R	

Here's the same rhythm with touches added. It's a little harder to play this way, but it has a fuller sound:

Rhythm 6-5: Bomba low drum part

1	+	2	+	3	+	4	+	1	+	2	+	3	+	4	+
△	•	•	O	•	O	O	•	△	•	•	O	O	O	O	•
R	L	R	L	R	L	R	L	R	L	R	L	R	L	R	L

Playing Principle
Keep your hands
close to the drumhead.

You'll find that you have to keep your hands close to the drumhead to play this rhythm fast. In fact, this is the safest and most efficient way to play all the time. Experienced drummers sometimes do raise their hands high in the air when they play a solo to increase volume or to create a dramatic effect. But extra arm motion can compromise speed and accuracy, and–especially with a beginner–can lead to injury. So play close, at least for now.

Playing Principle
Keep a steady tempo; don't
speed up when you play
louder or slow down when
you play softer.

Playing close will also help you maintain a steady tempo, which is far more important than speed. Afro-Cuban rhythms are generally played at an unvarying tempo, unless the leader of a group signals otherwise. So whatever speed you start with, learn to keep it steady for as long as you play a rhythm. In particular, try to resist the natural tendency to speed up when you play louder or slow down when you play softer.

5

Bembe rhythms in six

What we're calling rhythms in six are rhythms that can be counted in measures of six beats each. For those of us raised in the rock and pop world of four, the Afro-Cuban world of six is uncharted territory. Before we started drumming, we didn't even know this world existed; to us rhythms in six meant weddings, waltzes, and cold macaroni salads. But beyond our experience, hidden from view like the unconscious from the conscious mind, lay another world of six: deep, hypnotic, subtle, and powerful.

**Before we started drumming,
rhythms in six meant weddings, waltzes,
and cold macaroni salads.**

To introduce you to this world of six, we use bembe (bem-BAY) rhythms. Bembe, like rumba, refers to a family of Afro-Cuban rhythms, as well as to the gathering at which the rhythms are played. If you thought four was fun, wait till you try six. From the moment we started playing these bembe rhythms, we wanted to quit our jobs. We started hearing them coming from our clothes dryer. Then our car began idling in six, and before we knew it the windshield wipers were playing along. Now it's your turn. Don't say we didn't warn you.

Lesson 7

Tumbao in six and the bass-toe

The first basic bembe rhythm you're going to play is a six version of the tumbao pattern. When a heel-toe is taken out of tumbao, the pattern takes up 6 eighth notes instead of 8. Remember to lift the left hand off the drum after the touch on beat 4 for the open tones in the right hand on 5 and 6:

Rhythm 7-1: Tumbao in six

1	2	3	4	5	6
⌓	•	△	•	○	○
L	L	R	L	R	R

Musical Time-Out: Counting in six

Most of the rhythms in six in this book are charted in 6/8 time. That means there are 6 eighth notes to a measure and each eighth note gets one beat. In a two-measure rhythm in six, there are 12 eighth-note beats. Often those 12 beats could logically be charted in other ways. We chose 6/8 because that usually makes the rhythms easiest to understand and learn, and because that's how these rhythms are usually charted.

This is an easy rhythm to get lost in if you play it for a long time without thinking. It starts to feel like a circle after a while, with no clear beginning or ending. Getting lost in a rhythm can be a pleasant, hypnotic experience if it happens when you're playing alone. But when you lose track of 1 while playing with others, it can be unsettling and cause you to mess up your part.

Playing Principle
Always know where 1 is.

So you must always know where 1 is in any rhythm. For now, keep track of it by counting "1-2-3-4-5-6" as you play. Or say 1 each time it comes around. Or stomp your foot on 1. Or grunt. Or give in to the universal rhythmic reflex:

the funky chicken neck motion. Keep track of 1 in whatever way works for you.

If you have a drum machine, you can program a rhythm that has a loud sound on 1 and a quieter sound on the other counted beats: "BOOM-click-click-click-click-click." Besides giving you a reference point, the drum machine will also train you to keep steady time.

We don't recommend that you practice with a drum machine all the time. Its digital precision becomes monotonous after a while and can stifle feeling. Don't spend your whole practice session strapped into a musical straitjacket. Give yourself a chance to develop an internal sense of time.

One way to emphasize the 1 in this bembe rhythm is to convert the heel on 1 to a bass tone. This change makes the first two beats bass-toe instead of heel-toe:

Rhythm 7-2: Tumbao in six (variation)

1	2	3	4	5	6
✳	•	△	•	○	○
L	L	R	L	R	R

Any time you want to emphasize a beat with a heel stroke on it, you can convert the heel to a bass tone.

Practice Principle
Play along with a drum machine occasionally to give yourself a reference rhythm and to learn to keep steady time.

Playing Principle
Emphasize heel strokes by converting them to bass tones.

**Give in to the universal rhythmic reflex:
the funky chicken neck motion.**

Lesson 8

Bembe low and high drum parts

The low, middle, and high drum parts you're going to learn in the next two lessons are often combined when three drummers play bembe. In this lesson, you're going to learn two of the three parts.

Here's the low drum part. Remember to leave the left hand on the drumhead while you play the slap in the right and lift the left hand before you play the open tones in the right:

Rhythm 8-1: Bembe low drum part

1	2	3	4	5	6
✳	△		✳	○	○
L	R		L	R	R

Now here's the high drum part. Start by playing the part with open tones in your right hand and slaps in your left. Count while you play at first:

Rhythm 8-2: Bembe high drum part

1	2	3	4	5	6
○	△		○	△	
R	L		R	L	

You can also reverse your hands and play the open tone with the left and the slap with the right:

Rhythm 8-3: Bembe high drum part

1	2	3	4	5	6
O	△		O	△	
L	R		L	R	

Or you can alternate how you play each tone-slap combination:

Rhythm 8-4: Bembe high drum part

1	2	3	4	5	6
O	△		O	△	
R	L		L	R	

You'll probably find that if you play this bembe part in a group and play the slap with the same hand every time, that hand is going to get tired and sore after a while. That's why it's good to know how to play this rhythm in more than one way.

Learn to play both right-handed and left-handed on as many rhythms as possible. Play all the notes that were played by the right hand in the left, and vice versa. This will help prevent you from becoming a lopsided player, with one hand lagging behind the other in development. It will also equalize the wear and tear on your hands and save you from the pain that can result from repetitive motion.

Practice Principle
Learn to play both right-handed and left-handed on as many rhythms as possible.

Lesson 9

Bembe middle drum part and the drop

In this lesson, you're going to learn a middle drum part for bembe and a stroke we call the drop stroke. The drop stroke is so simple you don't even need an illustration. All you do is drop your hand gently to the drumhead.

The drop is like a touch done with the whole hand instead of just the fingertips and it serves some of the same functions as the touch: it keeps the hands flowing and keeps time. It also can be used to get the hand in position to muffle the head for a slap in the other hand. Whatever it's used for, it's always a soft stroke; it should barely be heard.

Memory Tip
The symbol for the drop stroke is a combination of the symbols for the heel and toe, both of which make contact with the drumhead in the drop.

When you play a drop stroke, your hand should be relaxed. If it is, it will naturally make contact with the head at the base of the palm and the fingertips. That's why the symbol for the drop is a combination of the symbols for heel and toe.

In the bembe middle drum part that follows, the drop falls on 4. The left hand comes up after beat 2 for the open tone in the right hand on 3. Then it drops down gently on 4 so it's in position to muffle the head for the slap in the right hand on 5:

Rhythm 9-1: Bembe middle drum part

1	2	3	4	5	6
᪥	•	◯	᪥	△	•
L	L	R	L	R	L

With a couple friends, you can now put this middle drum part together with the low drum part (Rhythm 8-1) and high drum part (Rhythm 8-2) you learned in the last lesson.

The next rhythm is an alternate way to play this middle drum part. The only difference you'll hear between the two is the bass tone in place of the open tone on beat 3 in the alternate version. But this substitution requires a couple subtle changes in the left hand:

Rhythm 9-2: Bembe middle drum part

1	2	3	4	5	6
ᴗ	•	✳	•	△	•
L	L	R	L	R	L

Since the open tones you play form the melody of a rhythm, substituting bass tones for open tones will change that melody. This is a common way that drummers vary their parts when playing in a group. It makes a rhythm less dense and repetitious without affecting its basic structure. You can experience the effect of substituting a bass tone for an open tone by combining Rhythms 9-1 and 9-2 and alternating between them:

Playing Principle
To make your part less dense, replace open tones with bass tones.

Rhythm 9-3: Bembe combined middle drum part

1	2	3	4	5	6	1	2	3	4	5	6
ᴗ	•	◯	ᴗ̇	△	•	ᴗ	•	✳	•	△	•
L	L	R	L	R	L	L	L	R	L	R	L

Lesson 10

Bembe middle drum part variations

In the last lesson, to create Rhythm 9-2 you substituted a bass tone for the open tone in Rhythm 9-1. In this lesson, you're going to use Rhythm 9-2 as home base and build variations off of it. Here it is again:

Rhythm 9-2: Bembe middle drum part

1	2	3	4	5	6
⌒	•	✳	•	△	•
L	L	R	L	R	L

Because this rhythm has no open tones, when it's played in a group it will add fullness to the underlying groove without calling attention to itself. Often, however, a drummer playing a part like this will have freedom to vary it. But the freedom is not unlimited.

Playing variations in Afro-Cuban rhythms isn't the same as jamming, where every musician is free to invent a part. Each player must reach a compromise between discipline and self-expression, community and individuality. When you're playing in a group, don't vary your part beyond what you're sure is acceptable. If you're not sure what's acceptable, ask. If you don't have a chance to ask, play your part without variation.

Group Playing Principle
Don't vary your part beyond what you're sure is acceptable.

The following rhythms are examples of generally acceptable variations that fit with the other bembe drum parts, and enliven the rhythm without overpowering it. Variation 1 has an open tone in the right hand on beat 1. The left hand, which usually plays on 1, now has to wait until beat 2 to drop to the head:

Rhythm 10-1: Bembe middle drum part, variation 1

1	2	3	4	5	6
◯	◌̇	✳	•	△	•
R	L	R	L	R	L

To hear how variation 1 functions, play it once followed immediately by three repetitions of Rhythm 9-2, and then repeat this four-measure pattern over and over without stopping.

Variation 2 has three open tones in a row. It has an open tone on beat 1, like variation 1, and also has two open tones on beats 5 and 6 of the preceding measure:

Rhythm 10-2: Bembe middle drum part, variation 2

5	6	1	2	3	4	5	6
○	○	○	⊖̇	✳	•	△	•
R	L	R	L	R	L	R	L

Here's how to insert variation 2 when you're playing the bembe middle drum part. Play three repetitions of Rhythm 9-2. Then on beat 5 of the fourth repetition, begin variation 2. The last of the three open tones you'll hear falls on beat 1, and marks the beginning of a new cycle.

Now that you know two variations, insert them while playing Rhythm 9-2. If you play these variations in a group, don't insert them at random. Unless a rhythm has a special arrangement, play your variations at regular intervals: every 2, 4, 8, or 16 repetitions. That way other players will be able to anticipate them and adapt their parts to complement yours.

Each player must reach a compromise between discipline and self-expression, community and individuality.

6

The clave

The clave (CLAH-vay) is at the heart of Afro-Cuban music. It
is a fundamental rhythmic pattern upon which other
rhythms are built.

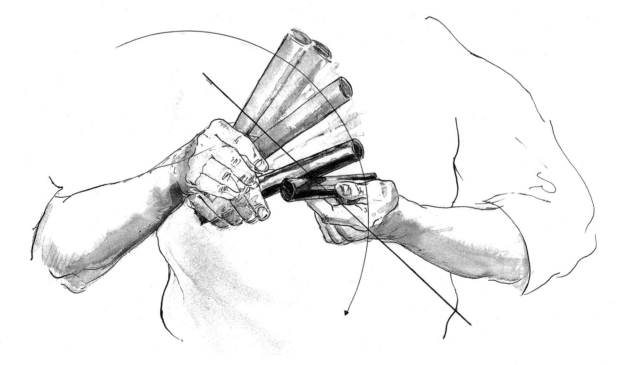

A clave pattern is usually played on two cylindrical pieces of wood called claves. Striking one against the other in the manner shown on the opposite page produces a crisp, penetrating sound that can be heard above all other instruments. Notice in the illustration that there is space between the bottom clave and the palm of the hand holding it. This channel allows the clave to resonate.

All the players in a group use the clave pattern as a reference rhythm and play their parts in relation to it. When you play in a group, you must learn to listen to the clave to keep your place. If you drift off and get lost, the clave will help you find your way back.

Group Playing Principle
Listen to the clave to keep your place.

Because everyone uses the clave pattern as a reference, playing it in a group is a big responsibility. From just listening to the clave, you may get the impression that playing it is simple. But it's a challenge that takes tremendous concentration. The clave pattern must be precisely played without variation for as long as a rhythm continues. Sometimes this can be for an hour or more.

Group Playing Principle
Play the clave pattern without variation.

When someone hands you the claves in a group, you'll immediately feel how challenging it is to hold the pattern steady. The complex weave of parts played by the instruments around you will compete for your attention or turn the rhythm around in your head. And there will be other distractions. Your nose will start to itch. Sweat will start to run into your eyes. Your hands will start to tire. But when you're on clave, you can't stop and you can't waiver. Everyone's counting on you.

Because the clave is the foundation of Afro-Cuban rhythms, some drum schools require beginners to master it before they're allowed to even touch a drum. A teacher might test your mastery by playing complex rhythms against your clave pattern, believing that if you can't hold the clave steady, you aren't ready for the drum.

You started with the drum, but from here on the clave is going to assume the central role it deserves. In this chapter, you're going to learn the three most common clave patterns: the one-bar clave, the son (SOHN) clave, and the rumba clave. After learning these claves, you're going to continue to work with them in a variety of ways. Whenever a rhythm has a clave–or another reference rhythm–you'll learn how your drum part fits with it. Eventually, these claves will become second nature.

Playing Afro-Cuban rhythms without knowing the clave is like jumping out of an airplane without a parachute; you'll make a big impression, but not the kind you want. You can spot the players in a group who don't know the clave: they're the ones who are always getting lost.

Even though we love the drum, we're happy to put it aside for a chance to play clave in a group. Playing clave builds rhythmic accuracy and steadiness like no other experience. And it puts you at the center of a rhythm, the perfect spot for hearing everything around you. If you want to be a good drummer, learn to play clave well.

Playing Afro-Cuban rhythms without knowing the clave is like jumping out of an airplane without a parachute; you'll make a big impression, but not the kind you want.

Lesson 11

The claves in tone-touch form

To learn the three clave patterns in this chapter, you're going to start by playing each in tone-touch form on the drum. After you learn how to play them on the drum, it will be much easier for you to play them with accuracy on the claves themselves.

When you play a rhythm in tone-touch form, you play the notes of the rhythm as open tones and the silent beats in between as touches. By playing a stroke on every beat, you'll be sure to put the notes of the rhythm in exactly the right places. You will also develop a felt sense for the length of time between notes. Your musicianship will deepen as you develop the ability not only to make the right sound at the

right moment but also to feel the silences between sounds.
The clave patterns are perfect for developing this ability
because of their open, asymmetrical structure. They're also
a delight to play because they punctuate silence in exquisite
and unexpected ways.

Your musicianship will deepen as you
develop the ability not only to make
the right sound at the right moment
but also to feel the silences
between sounds.

The first clave you're going to learn is the one-bar clave, a
pattern used in many Afro-Cuban rhythms. Here it is in
tone-touch form. There are three notes in the one-bar clave:
on 1, the AND of 2, and 4. Those notes are the open tones in
the following rhythm:

Rhythm 11-1: One-bar clave in tone-touch form

1	+	2	+	3	+	4	+
O	●	●	O	●	●	O	●
R	L	R	L	R	L	R	L

Notice as you play that the right hand plays each on-beat–
1, 2, 3, and 4–and the left hand plays each off-beat–the ANDs
of 1, 2, 3, and 4. Playing any rhythm in tone-touch form
drills into your body which notes are on-beats and which are
off-beats.

Make sure you clearly differentiate between tones and
touches. When you're comfortable with the rhythm,
concentrate on keeping the open tones strong while making
the touches as soft as possible. This will make the clave
really stand out, and help you learn the sound of the clave as
well as the feel. Let your hands teach your ears.

Although the three notes in the one-bar clave are evenly spaced in relation to each other, the clave becomes asymmetrical when it is repeated:

1	+	2	+	3	+	4	+	1	+	2	+	3	+	4	+
X			X			X		X			X			X	

As you can see just by looking at the pattern, when it repeats, the space between the note on 4 and the note on 1 is smaller than the space between the other notes. If the notes of a clave pattern were evenly spaced like the clicks of a metronome, it would be hard to tell where the pattern started or ended. When the notes are unevenly spaced, it's easy to tell where the pattern begins and easy to find your place if you get lost. For example, you can find the beginning of the one-bar clave by listening for the two notes that are closer together. The second of those two notes is 1.

The next clave is the son clave. It's two measures long. The first measure is the one-bar clave you just learned. The second measure contains two additional notes, which both fall on on-beats. Here it is in tone-touch form:

Rhythm 11-2: Son clave in tone-touch form

1	+	2	+	3	+	4	+	1	+	2	+	3	+	4	+
O	•	•	O	•	•	O	•	•	•	O	•	O	•	•	•
R	L	R	L	R	L	R	L	R	L	R	L	R	L	R	L

Practice the son clave in tone-touch form the same way you did the one-bar clave. Clearly differentiate the touches and tones. Then soften the touches and bring out the tones.

Now you're you're ready to learn the most challenging of the three claves: the rumba clave. Here it is in tone-touch form:

Rhythm 11-3: Rumba clave in tone-touch form

1	+	2	+	3	+	4	+	1	+	2	+	3	+	4	+
O	•	•	O	•	•	•	O	•	•	O	•	O	•	•	•
R	L	R	L	R	L	R	L	R	L	R	L	R	L	R	L

The rumba clave is the same as the son clave except for one note: the third one. It's played on the AND of 4, one eighth-note beat later than the third note of the son clave. This doesn't look like much of a difference on the page. But after you've worked with these two claves for a while, you'll see that this shift of a single note makes a world of difference in the way the two rhythms feel.

Musical Time-Out: Beats and eighth-note beats

Once each quarter note is divided into two eighth notes, it can become confusing whether the word "beat" means an eighth note or a quarter note. We avoid this confusion by always talking about eighth-note beats, as in "one eighth-note beat later."

We had a hard time playing the rumba clave correctly when we first learned it. We didn't know exactly where to put that third note, and usually played it a little too early or a little too late. Now we can see why. Not only does that third note fall on an off-beat, it's a long way from the second note, which is itself an off-beat. It's hard for a beginner to keep steady time between two widely-spaced off-beats.

But you're not going to have any problem learning the rumba clave. That's because, unlike us, you're learning it first in tone-touch form. You aren't going to have to guess where that third note is. Keeping your hands playing every beat evenly will guarantee that you'll put every note exactly where it's supposed to be in all three claves.

Lesson 12

The claves in pure form and the calypso low drum part

Now it's time to take off the training wheels and play the claves in pure form. You're going to start with the one-bar clave. It's the clave used in calypso, where the low drum part follows it note for note. So when you play the following low drum part from calypso, you're playing the rhythm of the one-bar clave in pure form:

Rhythm 12-1: Calypso low drum part

1	+	2	+	3	+	4	+
✳			✳			O	
L			R			R	

Playing Principle
Keep time with your feet.

Now you're going to do the son and rumba claves in pure form by omitting the touches you played when you first learned these claves in tone-touch form. Most people are a little wobbly when they first take off their training wheels, so you're going to use your feet to help you stay on course. Now is the time to get in the habit of keeping a pulse going in your feet when you play. Even experienced drummers do it.

While you're sitting, it may be easier to keep the ball of your foot on the floor and lift the heel. The heel comes down on the beat. But if you prefer tapping your toe, fine. Do that. In fast rhythms, you'll probably need to alternate feet. In slow rhythms, one foot is enough. Experiment. Do whatever feels natural, but keep a pulse going on the floor.

Tap your foot on every numbered beat as you play the son clave in pure form as open tones. The Xs on the chart show when to tap. We've switched the hand pattern so that you play all the notes with just your right hand because that's how you'd play the rhythm on the claves themselves:

Rhythm 12-2: Son clave

1	+	2	+	3	+	4	+	1	+	2	+	3	+	4	+
O			O			O				O		O			
R			R			R				R		R			
X		X		X		X		X		X		X		X	

Notice that when a note in the clave falls on an on-beat, hand and foot go down together. When the note falls on an off-beat–as it does on the AND of 2 in the first measure–your hand goes down while your foot comes up.

Next do the rumba clave the same way:

Rhythm 12-3: Rumba clave

1	+	2	+	3	+	4	+	1	+	2	+	3	+	4	+
O		O				O				O		O			
R		R				R				R		R			
X		X		X		X		X		X		X			

To make sure you've mastered both of these claves, alternate playing them without stopping. Make sure you're placing the third note of each clave in the right spot: on 4 in the son clave and on the AND of 4 in the rumba clave.

When the pace picks up, it becomes difficult and tiring to tap your foot on every beat. So now tap on every other beat, with your heel or toe hitting the floor on 1 and 3 of each measure. Do the son clave this way first:

Rhythm 12-4: Son clave

1	+	2	+	3	+	4	+	1	+	2	+	3	+	4	+
O			O			O					O		O		
R			R			R					R		R		
X				X				X				X			

Now do the rumba clave this way:

Rhythm 12-5: Rumba clave

1	+	2	+	3	+	4	+	1	+	2	+	3	+	4	+
O			O				O				O		O		
R			R				R				R		R		
X				X				X				X			

Notice that in both claves, your hand and foot strike together on the first and last note of the pattern. These spots are little oases on each side of the clave where you can pull yourself together for the more difficult journey between them.

If you've worked through this chapter systematically, we know your clave notes are going to be in the right places. If you get together to play with a group and someone hands you the claves, you should feel comfortable and confident. You've become someone others can depend on for rhythmic steadiness. You're about to become popular.

Lesson 13

The rumba clave in the palito patterns

"Palito" (pah-LEE-toh) means little stick in Spanish. Palito patterns are traditionally played with sticks on a hard surface such as a hollow wood block or the side of a drum. Palito patterns contain the notes of the rumba clave within them and can be played with many Afro-Cuban rhythms.

Play the first palito pattern with slaps. We've added the rumba clave to the chart of this palito pattern by using circles on the count row. From now on, all the clave patterns will be indicated in this way. Notice that the right hand tracks the clave note for note:

Rhythm 13-1: Palito pattern 1

1	+	2	+	3	+	4	+	1	+	2	+	3	+	4	+
△			△	△		△			△	△		△	△		△
R		L	R		L		R	L		R		R	L		L

To make sure you know where the clave is, play the pattern again, this time using slaps in the right hand and touches in the left:

Rhythm 13-2: Palito pattern 1

1	+	2	+	3	+	4	+	1	+	2	+	3	+	4	+
△		•	△		•		△	•		△		△	•		•
R		L	R		L		R	L		R		R	L		L

In the next palito pattern, the right hand plays steadily on beats 1 and 3 in each measure. Start by doing the whole pattern with slaps:

Rhythm 13-3: Palito pattern 2

1	+	2	+	3	+	4	+	1	+	2	+	3	+	4	+
△	△		△	△	△		△	△		△		△	△		△
R	L		L	R	L		L	R		L		R	L		L

If you have trouble remembering this pattern, think of it as four equal sections of 4 eighth notes each. Notice that the first, second, and fourth sections are identical. Only the third section is different.

Playing Principle
Strive to make each technique sound the same in both hands.

Playing these palito patterns is good practice for your slap technique. Focus on making the slaps sound the same in your weak hand as they do in your strong hand. Strive to make every technique sound the same in both hands. A listener shouldn't be able to tell which hand is playing.

Lesson 14

Saying the claves and playing tumbao

The best way to learn how a rhythm fits with the clave is to say the clave while you play the rhythm. Doing this drives the clave deep into your unconscious. Experienced drummers feel the clave internally, even when no one's playing it. That's how they're able to play complicated solos or embellishments and still come back in exactly the right place. The more you say the clave while you play, the less likely it is that you'll get lost in a rhythm and the more secure you'll be when you play in a group.

In this lesson, you're going to say each of the three clave patterns you've learned while playing a rhythm you already know: tumbao. Tumbao is traditionally played with the son clave, but we chose it for this exercise because–of all the hand patterns you already know–it's the easiest to play with all three claves.

Start with the one-bar clave. Choose a syllable for the clave notes that you can say quickly and crisply, like "KA." Cut each syllable short, so it doesn't extend into the next beat.

Before you start to play, notice which strokes in tumbao the clave notes fall on. After the first beat, the notes of the one-bar clave fall on the toe in the left hand on the AND of 2, and on the open tone in the right hand on 4. Memorize how the clave fits with the hand strokes. Then you can abandon the chart and watch your hands to cue yourself on when to say the clave notes:

Rhythm 14-1: Tumbao and the one-bar clave

1	+	2	+	3	+	4	+
KA			KA			KA	
◡	•	△	•	◡	•	○	○
L	L	R	L	L	L	R	R

Next say the son clave while playing tumbao. Because the son clave takes up two measures, you'll have to play the tumbao pattern twice while saying the clave once. That means that the clave notes in the second measure won't fit with tumbao in the same way as they did in the first measure. The first measure is the same as the one-bar clave with tumbao, but the second measure is new:

Rhythm 14-2: Tumbao and the son clave

1	+	2	+	3	+	4	+	1	+	2	+	3	+	4	+
KA			KA			KA					KA		KA		
◡	•	△	•	◡	•	○	○	◡	•	△	•	◡	•	○	○
L	L	R	L	L	L	R	R	L	L	R	L	L	L	R	R

Finally, say the rumba clave while playing tumbao. The only
difference between this combination and the tumbao-son
clave combination is in where you say the third note of the
clave. The third note now falls on the second of the two
open tones:

Rhythm 14-3: Tumbao and the rumba clave

1	+	2	+	3	+	4	+	1	+	2	+	3	+	4	+
KA		KA				KA				KA		KA			
◡	•	△	•	◡	•	○	○	◡	•	△	•	◡	•	○	○
L	L	R	L	L	L	R	R	L	L	R	L	L	L	R	R

Practice Principle
*Say the clave while playing a
new rhythm to learn exactly
how they fit together.*

Practice Principle
*Learn a few rhythms well
rather than many
superficially.*

From now on, one of your first steps in learning any rhythm
that has a clave part should be to play the rhythm slowly
while saying the clave. When you can do this with ease, you
can stop saying the clave out loud and let it continue to play
internally.

There's no question that learning to say the clave while you
play will reduce the rate at which you can learn new
rhythms. But it's essential to building your depth as a
player. Don't play a mile wide and an inch deep. Learn a
few rhythms well.

We know the temptation to learn as many rhythms as
possible as fast as possible. They're like narcotics; the more
you get, the more you want. Before you know it, you're a
rhythm junkie, trying to score one wherever you can. We
admit we were once powerless over our urge to learn to play
everything we heard. With help from our teachers, we are
now on the path to recovery, one rhythm at a time.
KA, KA, KA . . . KA, KA.

Lesson 15

The 2-3 rumba clave and conga

The rhythm called conga is often played with the rumba
clave. In this lesson, you're going to learn how to start the
two-measure pattern of the rumba clave in the second
measure instead of the first, because that's how it's played
with conga.

The measure you know as the first measure of the rumba
clave has three notes in it; the measure you know as the
second has two. The measure with three notes is called the
3-side of the clave; the measure with two notes is called the
2-side. When the 3-side comes first and the 2-side comes
second, the pattern is called a 3-2 rumba clave:

3-2 rumba clave

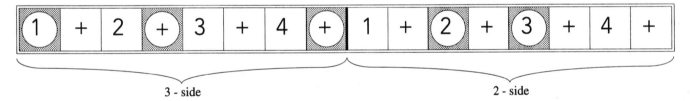

In many Afro-Cuban rhythms and songs, the 2-side of the
clave comes first and the 3-side comes second. When the
rumba clave is played that way, it's called the 2-3 rumba
clave:

2-3 rumba clave

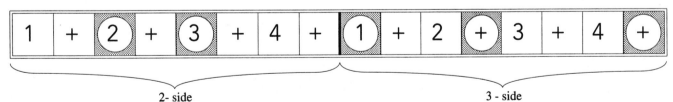

Conga is based on a 2-3 rumba clave. Here's the conga high
drum part you learned in Lesson 2 with the clave pattern
added in the count row. Say the clave while you play the
part. Notice that nothing happens until beat 2, so you need

to do something to mark beat 1. We like to grunt on 1, but if that's not your style, try tapping your foot:

Rhythm 15-1: Conga high drum part with clave

1	+	2	+	3	+	4	+	1	+	2	+	3	+	4	+
		△	△			O	O			△	△			O	O
		R	L			R	L			R	L			R	L

Once you get going, you'll probably drift back into feeling the 3-side as the beginning of the pattern. This is natural because the 3-side has a note on 1. Without having other instruments or a vocal line to reinforce the feel of the 2-side as the beginning of the pattern, it's easy to get turned around. When you play in a group and hear your part as part of a song, the 2-side will stay put.

Now you're ready for the rest of the conga drum parts. Since these patterns are more challenging, start by just playing each of them without saying the clave. When you get comfortable with each part, add the clave:

Rhythm 15-2: Conga low drum part

1	+	2	+	3	+	4	+	1	+	2	+	3	+	4	+
✳				✳				✳			O				
R				R				R			R				

1	+	2	+	3	+	4	+	1	+	2	+	3	+	4	+
✳		✳		✳		✳		✳			O				
R		R		R		R		R			R				

Rhythm 15-3: Conga middle drum part

1	+	2	+	3	+	4	+	1	+	2	+	3	+	4	+
O			O	△		△			O		O	△		△	
R			L	R		L			R		L	R		L	

Rhythm 15-4: Conga middle drum part

1	+	2	+	3	+	4	+	1	+	2	+	3	+	4	+
O		△		△			O	O			△	△		△	
R		L		R			L	R			L	R		L	

Now you've got four drum parts for conga plus the clave. They're all right here. If you haven't played with others yet, now's the time. Create a study group. Cook up a pot of chili and invite everyone over. When you put these parts together, and the rhythm starts to percolate, it'll be hard to get your friends out the door.

If you don't have any playing partners, you can tape yourself playing each part and then play along with your recording. Recording yourself is good for a lot of reasons. It allows you to hear how you sound from the outside and frees you to concentrate on just listening to yourself without having to divide your attention between listening and playing. When you hear yourself on tape, it's easy to pick out slaps that aren't even and tempos that fluctuate. Face the music. Hiding from your weaknesses only guarantees that you'll strengthen them.

Practice Principle
Record yourself.

But recording isn't just good for finding fault. If you date and keep the tapes, they'll provide evidence of your progress for those frustrating days when you can't remember you've made any. Instead of comparing yourself to other drummers who started before you did or who catch on faster, compare yourself to yourself a year ago. Celebrate your own progress.

7

Heel–toe patterns

You first encountered heel-toe patterns back in Chapter 1
when you learned what a heel and toe were. Since then,
you've only played heel and toe strokes with your left hand.
In this chapter, you're going to play them with both hands in
patterns which form the foundation of a wide variety of
rhythms.

Heel-toe patterns are great warm-ups; the relaxed, galloping
motions are gentle on the hands and soothing to the ear.
They're satisfying to play when you're alone because the
fullness of the patterns makes one drum sound like many.
And they serve as a good home base for improvisation
because your hands always have something to do while you
wait for inspiration.

Lesson 16

The heel-heel-toe-toe pattern

Since many rhythms require a fast rocking of the hands,
we've chosen a basic heel-toe pattern to get you started. In
the first rhythm, you're going to be playing twice as fast in
the first measure as in the second. It's like doing wind
sprints: you sprint the first half and then jog the second to
catch your breath:

Rhythm 16-1: Heel-toe pattern 1

1	+	2	+	3	+	4	+	1	+	2	+	3	+	4	+
⌣	⌣	●	●	⌣	⌣	●	●	⌣		⌣		●		●	
R	L	R	L	R	L	R	L	R		L		R		L	

Now try increasing the distance:

Rhythm 16-2: Heel-toe pattern 2

1	+	2	+	3	+	4	+	1	+	2	+	3	+	4	+
⌣	⌣	●	●	⌣	⌣	●	●	⌣	⌣	●	●	⌣	⌣	●	●
R	L	R	L	R	L	R	L	R	L	R	L	R	L	R	L

1	+	2	+	3	+	4	+	1	+	2	+	3	+	4	+
⌣		⌣		●		●		⌣		⌣		●		●	
R		L		R		L		R		L	R	R		L	

You've probably noticed that as your speed and the length of your sprint increase, it gets harder and harder to keep the pattern even. Whenever you find your hands flopping around like fish on the drumhead, it's time to slow down.

In the next rhythm, you sprint from start to finish. It's all heels and toes without a break, except that it starts with two open tones that take the place of the first two heels. When you play the pattern over and over at high speed, the tones act as reference points, breaking the uniformity of the rhythm and allowing you to get your bearings. They also give your hands a chance to release any tension that may have built up during the heel-toe part of the pattern:

Rhythm 16-3: Heel-toe pattern 3

1	+	2	+	3	+	4	+	1	+	2	+	3	+	4	+
O	O	•	•	⌓	⌓	•	•	⌓	⌓	•	•	⌓	⌓	•	•
R	L	R	L	R	L	R	L	R	L	R	L	R	L	R	L

**Whenever you find your hands
flopping around like fish on the drumhead,
it's time to slow down.**

---

*Playing Principle
Play relaxed.*

Now use this same rhythm as a way to check in with your body. Play at the fastest speed you can maintain for at least three minutes. A couple minutes into the pattern, focus on the muscles in your face. Is your jaw relaxed? How about your neck and shoulders? Now move down your arms. Are they relaxed? Are your wrists loose? Wherever you encounter tension on this route, consciously release it. To play fast, to play long, to play well–play relaxed.

*Playing Principle
Breathe naturally.*

Next check your breathing. Are you breathing? Good. When we first started drumming, as soon as we had to play something fast or difficult, our lungs would shut down as if we were underwater. As soon as we came up for air, our playing improved. Make sure that your breathing always stays relaxed and regular, especially when you're under pressure.

Lesson 17

Rumba middle drum part and variations

The basic heel-toe pattern you just worked on forms the foundation of a middle drum part for rumba. In this lesson, you're going to learn that part and three variations on it.

The basic part has two measures. The first measure is pure
heel-toe. The second measure is the same except for an
open tone on 1 and a silent beat on the AND of 1:

Rhythm 17-1: Rumba middle drum part

1	+	2	+	3	+	4	+	1	+	2	+	3	+	4	+
◡	◡	•	•	◡	◡	•	•	◯		•	•	◡	◡	•	•
R	L	R	L	R	L	R	L	R		R	L	R	L	R	L

When you're playing this rhythm, you have to stay alert to
keep track of where it starts. Because the open tone stands
out, it's easy to get turned around and mistake it for the
beginning of the pattern. The best way to avoid this is to say
the clave with it. When you can play this part and say the
clave at the same time, playing the part in a group will be
easy. In a group, all you'll have to do is listen for the clave
because someone else will be playing it.

Now you're ready to play some variations. When you played
variations on other rhythms, you inserted a variation at
regular intervals, such as every four repetitions. Do the same
here. Play the basic part for three repetitions, and then play
the following variation in place of the fourth repetition. It's
got three open tones instead of just one:

Rhythm 17-2: Rumba middle drum part, variation 1

1	+	2	+	3	+	4	+	1	+	2	+	3	+	4	+
◯		•	•	◯		•	•	◯		•	•	◡	◡	•	•
R		R	L	R		R	L	R		R	L	R	L	R	L

Here's the second variation. Insert it in place of every fourth
repetition of the basic part. It's got five open tones:

Rhythm 17-3: Rumba middle drum part, variation 2

1	+	2	+	3	+	4	+	1	+	2	+	3	+	4	+
O	O	•	•	O	O	•	•	O		•	•	◡	◡	•	•
R	L	R	L	R	L	R	L	R		R	L	R	L	R	L

Finally, here's the third variation. Insert it every fourth repetition. It's got three open tones, but notice that the first open tone falls on beat 3 of the first measure. It's the same as variation 2 minus the first two open tones. Make sure you keep track of 1 so that you don't play the first open tone in this variation too early:

Rhythm 17-4: Rumba middle drum part, variation 3

1	+	2	+	3	+	4	+	1	+	2	+	3	+	4	+
◡	◡	•	•	O	O	•	•	O		•	•	◡	◡	•	•
R	L	R	L	R	L	R	L	R		R	L	R	L	R	L

Group Playing Principle
No matter how simple or repetitive your part, play it as if the whole rhythm depended on it.

Now that you know this middle drum part for rumba, get a couple friends and put it together with the clave and the low drum part you learned in Lesson 3. You may already be at the point where that low drum part isn't challenging to play, even with others. But that doesn't mean you can just go on automatic pilot while you play it. Always put your heart into what you're playing. When played with good technique and true feeling, any part can be beautiful. No matter how simple or repetitive your part, play it as if the whole rhythm depended on it.

Lesson 18

Learning to improvise using heel-toe patterns

It's probably going to be a while before you're asked to play lead drum in a group, but it's never too soon to start learning to improvise. In this lesson, you're going to play variations on the heel-heel-toe-toe pattern that will give you ideas for variations of your own. As you work through them, you're going to be building a phrase note by note.

The groove of a heel-toe pattern provides a solid home base for improvisation. If you're nervous about improvising, the pattern will help you feel more secure because your hands always have something to do while you decide what to play next. And the steady pitter-patter of your hands creates the illusion that there's a band backing you while you take the lead.

The first variation is pure heel-toe except for an open tone in the left hand on the AND of 1 in the second measure. Make sure your right hand is off the drum when you play that open tone:

Rhythm 18-1: Heel-toe variation 1

1	+	2	+	3	+	4	+	1	+	2	+	3	+	4	+
⌣	⌣	●	●	⌣	⌣	●	●	⌣	○	●	●	⌣	⌣	●	●
R	L	R	L	R	L	R	L	R	L	R	L	R	L	R	L

Now add an open tone in the right hand on 1 of the first measure. Feel the contrast between the on-beat open tone in the right hand and the off-beat open tone in the left:

74   CONGA DRUMMING

Rhythm 18-2: Heel-toe variation 2

1	+	2	+	3	+	4	+	1	+	2	+	3	+	4	+
○	⌣	•	•	⌣	⌣	•	•	⌣	○	•	•	⌣	⌣	•	•
R	L	R	L	R	L	R	L	R	L	R	L	R	L	R	L

Now add a slap in the left hand on the AND of 2 in the second measure. This adds a little spice to the phrase:

Rhythm 18-3: Heel-toe variation 3

1	+	2	+	3	+	4	+	1	+	2	+	3	+	4	+
○	⌣	•	•	⌣	⌣	•	•	⌣	○	•	△	⌣	⌣	•	•
R	L	R	L	R	L	R	L	R	L	R	L	R	L	R	L

Finally, add another tone-slap combination in the left hand in the second measure:

Rhythm 18-4: Heel-toe variation 4

1	+	2	+	3	+	4	+	1	+	2	+	3	+	4	+
○	⌣	•	•	⌣	⌣	•	•	⌣	○	•	△	⌣	○	•	△
R	L	R	L	R	L	R	L	R	L	R	L	R	L	R	L

You can build your own musical phrases by this same process of gradual variation. Get your hands moving in a steady heel-toe pattern at a comfortable speed. At first, just venture out for a note or two, then scamper back to the basic pattern. Replace a heel with a tone, or a toe with a slap . As you get comfortable, gradually increase the amount of time you spend away from home. Whenever you get homesick, the groove will be there waiting for you.

The best way to get ideas for improvisation is to listen to lots of Afro-Cuban music and any other percussion music. Even if you aren't able to give the music your full attention, put it on in the background while you're driving or doing dishes so that your unconscious can absorb it. The subtleties of style, phrasing, and feel of Afro-Cuban rhythms cannot be written down and may not even be teachable. You have to experience them directly by listening to the playing of masters of the art.

Practice Principle:
Listen to lots of
Afro-Cuban music.

Lesson 19

The heel-toe-toe-heel pattern

In this lesson, you're going to work with a slightly different heel-toe pattern we call the heel-toe-toe-heel pattern:

Rhythm 19-1: Heel-toe-toe-heel pattern

1	+	2	+	3	+	4	+
◡	●	●	◡	◡	●	●	◡
R	L	R	L	R	L	R	L

As you play, you'll probably notice that your hands are once again making a heel-heel-toe-toe pattern, this time from left to right, starting with the left heel. Thinking of the pattern in this way may make it easier to learn, but you must remember that the left heel does not fall on 1; it falls on the AND of 4 just before 1. The right heel is 1.

Playing a different heel-toe pattern opens up new possibilities for variation. The following middle drum part from calypso is exactly the same as this new heel-toe pattern, except for the open tone in the left hand on the AND of 4:

Rhythm 19-2: Calypso middle drum part

1	+	2	+	3	+	4	+
⌣	•	•	⌣	⌣	•	•	◯
R	L	R	L	R	L	R	L

This part doesn't sound like much by itself, but it fits beautifully with the other middle drum part from calypso you learned in Chapter 1. You now know five parts for calypso: four drum parts and the one-bar clave. Get some friends and put them all together.

You can base improvisations off the heel-toe-toe-heel pattern just as you did off the other basic heel-toe pattern. The first variation here resembles the calypso middle drum part you just learned, but a slap is added in the second measure:

Rhythm 19-3: Heel-toe-toe-heel variation 1

1	+	2	+	3	+	4	+	1	+	2	+	3	+	4	+
⌣	•	•	⌣	⌣	•	•	◯	⌣	△	•	⌣	⌣	•	•	⌣
R	L	R	L	R	L	R	L	R	L	R	L	R	L	R	L

Next add an open tone in the right hand on 1 of the first measure:

Rhythm 19-4: Heel-toe-toe-heel variation 2

1	+	2	+	3	+	4	+	1	+	2	+	3	+	4	+
◯	•	•	⌣	⌣	•	•	◯	⌣	△	•	⌣	⌣	•	•	⌣
R	L	R	L	R	L	R	L	R	L	R	L	R	L	R	L

Finally, add a slap in the right hand after the open tone in the right hand. This should make it easy for you to feel the contrast between the on-beat tone-slap phrase in the right hand and the off-beat tone-slap phrase in the left:

Rhythm 19-5: Heel-toe-toe-heel variation 3

1	+	2	+	3	+	4	+	1	+	2	+	3	+	4	+
○	•	△	◡	◡	•	•	○	◡	△	•	◡	◡	•	•	◡
R	L	R	L	R	L	R	L	R	L	R	L	R	L	R	L

Now it's your turn to make up your own patterns.

After you've practiced these new rhythms, go back and review all the rhythms you've learned so far. In fact, it's always a good idea to include some review whenever you practice. You'll discover something new in these rhythms every time you play them. The feeling in your hands will be constantly changing as your technique improves. The way you hear will evolve as you gain experience and learn how rhythms fit together. New rhythms will appear within the hidden depths of the old.

As you build your repertoire of rhythms, you won't have time to review everything each time you practice. Cycle through the rhythms a few at a time, even if takes a week or a month to get through them all.

Try doing your review at different times in your practice sessions. Sometimes it feels good to start with a review. It's a relaxing way to warm up your hands. It also reminds you that you're competent before you tackle a new rhythm. On the other hand, sometimes it's best to start your practice session with a new rhythm, when you've got the most energy and greatest ability to concentrate. The review can then be a relaxing and satisfying way to end the session. Play around until you find what works best for you.

Practice Principle
Include some review whenever you practice.

Lesson 20

The claves in heel-toe form

In this lesson, you're going to review all three clave patterns by playing them in heel-toe form. Played in this way, the claves become like tongue twisters for the hands. And just as practicing tongue twisters improves articulation, playing the claves in this way improves dexterity. It also drives the clave patterns even deeper into your body while preparing you to play other variations on heel-toe patterns.

Playing a clave in heel-toe form is a lot like playing it in tone-touch form. Again you make the notes of the clave stand out by playing them as open tones. The only difference is that in heel-toe form you fill in all the spaces between the notes with heels and toes instead of just touches. Start with the one-bar clave. It's tricky, so take it slow:

Rhythm 20-1: One-bar clave in heel-toe form

1	+	2	+	3	+	4	+
O	◡	●	O	◡	◡	O	●
R	L	R	L	R	L	R	L

Now play the son clave in this form:

Rhythm 20-2: Son clave in heel-toe form

1	+	2	+	3	+	4	+	1	+	2	+	3	+	4	+
O	◡	●	O	◡	◡	O	●	◡	◡	O	●	O	◡	●	●
R	L	R	L	R	L	R	L	R	L	R	L	R	L	R	L

The key to playing this pattern correctly is getting the right heel on 1 of the second measure. You need to avoid the instinct to play a toe there.

Finally, play the rumba clave:

Rhythm 20-3: Rumba clave in heel-toe form

1	+	2	+	3	+	4	+	1	+	2	+	3	+	4	+
◯	⌣	•	◯	⌣	⌣	•	◯	⌣	⌣	◯	•	◯	⌣	•	•
R	L	R	L	R	L	R	L	R	L	R	L	R	L	R	L

Nice job! If you've taken the time to master these patterns, you're well on your way along the drummer's path. You've just finished the most challenging stretch of the journey so far. After a steep climb like this, it's good to catch your breath and take a look at where you are and how far you've come. Your body isn't the same as when you started. It's more alive and graceful. Your hands are dancing now.

8

Advanced rhythms in four

This chapter contains everything you need to fill out the rhythms in four you've learned. It starts with a lesson on the cowbell and the cowbell parts for calypso, bomba, and conga. Next come the more difficult drum parts for bomba and rumba. When you learn variations on the rumba low drum part, you'll learn to play the muffled tone, the only basic stroke you haven't learned yet.

The last lesson is a brief introduction to playing quinto. The quinto is the conga drum with the highest pitch, usually played by a lead drummer. Since lead drummers often solo on this drum, playing quinto also refers to soloing. In Lesson 25, you'll learn a basic quinto part for rumba.

Lesson 21

Cowbell parts for calypso, bomba, and conga

Like the click of the claves, the clear tone of the cowbell cuts through the sound of all other instruments. This means that when you play the cowbell you don't have to strain to be heard. But it also means that if you're off, it's going to be painfully obvious to everyone. That's why it's always puzzled us that often the first instrument handed to a beginner is the cowbell, while more experienced players are given drums. Although a beginner can usually produce a passable sound on the bell, unless the rhythm is played exactly in time it can throw off a whole group. If you ever notice four or five other players glaring in your direction, check to see if there's a cowbell in your hand.

The cowbell is held in one hand in front of the solar plexus and played with a stick held in the other hand, like the claves. The mouth of the bell should face away from you. Notice that when you're standing, the bell will be at ear level for a seated drummer. Since cowbell players often stand behind drummers and the bell has a piercing sound, it's important not to play the bell directly into someone's head. If you're right on the beat and you're still getting nasty looks, check the location of your bell.

There are two basic strokes on the cowbell. The first is the stroke on the mouth of the bell:

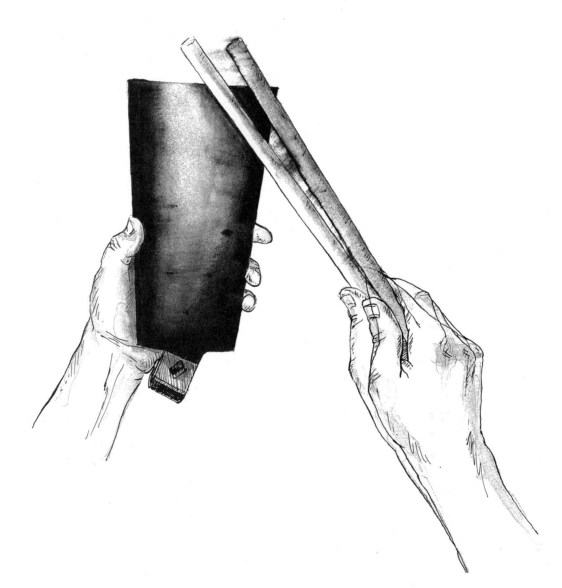

The other basic stroke is the stroke on the neck of the bell:

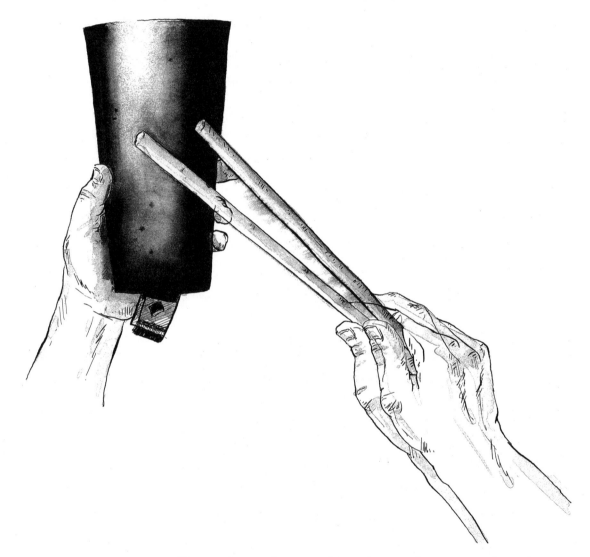

The stroke on the mouth produces a lower tone than the stroke on the neck. This difference in pitch makes it possible to play simple melodies on the bell.

If a bell is too loud for a particular playing situation, you can muffle the sound by stuffing something into it, like a piece of foam or a sock. You can also control the ringing of the bell by pressing and releasing your index finger on the underside of the bell.

**If you ever notice four or five other players
glaring in your direction, check to see
if there's a cowbell in your hand.**

To chart cowbell parts, we've divided the row under the count row in half. The two halves of each box correspond to the bell as it appears when you look down at it in your hand. An "X" in the upper half of a box indicates a stroke on the mouth of the bell; an "X" in the lower half indicates a stroke on the neck.

The first cowbell part you're going to learn is for calypso. It has strokes only on the neck of the bell. They fall on 2, the AND of 2, 4, and the AND of 4:

Rhythm 21-1: Calypso cowbell part

1	+	2	+	3	+	4	+	1	+	2	+	3	+	4	+
		X	X			X	X			X	X			X	X

This is a good all-purpose bell part that fits with many rhythms. If you don't know a bell part for a rhythm in four, try this one. You can also play bell strokes on beats 1 and 3 with just about any rhythm in four.

The cowbell part for bomba also has strokes only on the neck of the bell. Here are three variations:

Rhythm 21-2: Bomba cowbell part, variation 1

1	+	2	+	3	+	4	+	1	+	2	+	3	+	4	+
X		X	X		X	X		X		X	X		X	X	

Rhythm 21-3: Bomba cowbell part, variation 2

①	+	2	⊕	3	+	④	+	1	+	②	+	③	+	4	+
X	X		X		X	X		X	X		X		X	X	

Rhythm 21-4: Bomba cowbell part, variation 3

①	+	2	⊕	3	+	④	+	1	+	②	+	③	+	4	+
X	X		X	X	X	X		X	X		X	X	X	X	

The cowbell part for conga is more intricate and challenging than the bell parts you've learned so far. It dances around the clave, and together they are the driving force of the conga rhythm. It has strokes on both the neck and the mouth of the bell:

Rhythm 21-5: Conga cowbell part

1	+	②	+	③	+	4	+	①	+	2	+	3	⊕	4	⊕
X		X					X		X	X					
				X		X							X		X

To learn this cowbell part, it's helpful to sing it first. Sing low tones for the strokes on the mouth of the bell and higher tones for the strokes on the neck:

Rhythm 21-6: Conga cowbell part

1	+	②	+	③	+	4	+	①	+	2	+	3	⊕	4	⊕
LO		LO		HI	HI			LO		LO	LO		HI		HI

Singing or saying any rhythm is a great way to get to know it. If you can say it, you can play it.

Finally, to bring the dance of the cowbell and clave into your body, sing the cowbell part while clapping the clave. This is challenging, but you can do it if you break it down into pieces and learn a piece at a time. For example, this rhythm could be broken into three pieces: the first piece goes through beat 4 of the first measure, the second through the AND of 2 in the second measure, and the third is the rest. Practice each piece separately. Remember to go slow.

When you can do each piece separately, start putting them together. First put the first piece with the second. Then put the second with the third. Finally, put them all together. Then gradually speed up until the clave pattern becomes recognizable. When you've mastered the cowbell part, put it together with the drum parts for conga from Lesson 15 and the clave.

You've now been introduced to three instruments that are at the heart of Afro-Cuban rhythms: drum, clave, and cowbell. Many other percussion instruments are used in Afro-Cuban music which we don't cover in this book, including a beaded gourd called a shekere (sheh-keh-RAY) that is shaken, a grooved gourd called a guiro (GWEE-roh) that is scraped with a stick, a mounted piece of bamboo called a guagua (GWAH-gwah) that is played with sticks, and metal drums called timbales (teem-BAH-less) that are also played with sticks. Each has its own personality and unique sound, adding spice and color to the rhythms. Learn to play as many of these instruments as you can. Each offers a unique vantage point for experiencing the rhythms.

There are also practical reasons to learn other percussion instruments. Most of these instruments are easier to carry around than a drum, so you can take them wherever you go. You can toss a shekere into a small backpack and slip claves into a back pocket. You also may be able to play with more experienced musicians if you can play something besides a drum; you only need to know a few common clave and bell parts to play many Afro-Cuban rhythms. And your wrists and hands sometimes need a break from the repetitive movements of drumming. By cross-training with a variety of instruments, you can play longer without straining your body.

Practice Principle
If you can say it,
you can play it.

Practice Principle
Learn a difficult rhythm
a piece at a time.

Lesson 22

Bomba middle and high drum parts

Like most Afro-Cuban rhythms in four, bomba can be played with either the rumba clave or the son clave. Because we use the rumba clave with rumba and conga, we're presenting bomba with the son clave.

Also like many Afro-Cuban rhythms in four, bomba can be played so that it starts on either the 3-side or the 2-side of the clave. In this lesson, we present two pairs of bomba drum parts. When you play bomba using the first set of parts, the rhythm starts on the 3-side of the son clave; when you play bomba using the second set of parts, the rhythm starts on the 2-side. If this seems confusing, just study the clave patterns on the charts and it should become clear.

Playing Principle
Many Afro-Cuban rhythms in four can be started on either the 3-side or the 2-side of the clave.

The parts in this lesson go with the bomba low drum part that you learned in Lesson 6, as well as the cowbell parts you learned in Lesson 21. But each pair can stand alone as a simple duet because the parts complement each other so beautifully.

Here's the middle drum part from the first pair:

Rhythm 22-1: Bomba middle drum part

1	+	2	+	3	+	4	+	1	+	2	+	3	+	4	+
✳	•	•	△	✳	○	○	•	✳	•	•	△	✳	○	○	•
R	L	R	L	R	L	R	L	R	L	R	L	R	L	R	L

Notice that the open tone in the right hand on 4 is preceded by a bass tone in the right hand. When you play this rhythm fast, you have to play that open tone on the way back from the bass tone. Because this is a new move for your right hand, you may want to practice moving back and forth from a bass tone to an open tone until you get the feel of it.

Here's the high drum part from the first pair:

Rhythm 22-2: Bomba high drum part

1	+	2	+	3	+	4	+	1	+	2	+	3	+	4	+
✳	O	O	O	✳	•	•	△	✳	O	O	O	✳	•	•	△
R	L	R	L	R	L	R	L	R	L	R	L	R	L	R	L

The second pair of parts come from an African rhythm called illesa (ee-YEH-sah) that is often played with the bomba low drum part. When bomba is combined with these parts from illesa, the rhythm starts on the 2-side of the son clave. Here's the high drum part from illesa:

Rhythm 22-3: Illesa high drum part

1	+	2	+	3	+	4	+	1	+	2	+	3	+	4	+
△	•	⊔	•	⊔	•	O	⊙	△	•	⊔	•	O	⊙	O	⊙
R	L	L	L	L	L	R	L	R	L	L	L	R	L	R	L

Rhythm 22-4: Illesa middle drum part

1	+	2	+	3	+	4	+	1	+	2	+	3	+	4	+
O	⊙	O	△	⊔	•	△	⊔	•	O	⊙	△	⊔	•	△	⊙
R	L	R	R	L	L	R	L	L	R	L	R	L	L	R	L

Left hand: "Are you kidding me? For 27 years you don't even ask me to pick up a cup, and now you expect me to do *this*?" No matter what kind of complaints you get from your left hand, make sure it's rock steady. Even though the timekeeping strokes aren't as prominent as the slaps and tones in the right hand, they're the driving force behind the rhythm.

Left hand: "Are you kidding me? For 27 years you don't even ask me to pick up a cup, and now you expect me to do *this*?"

Lesson 23

Rumba low drum part variations and the muffled tone

In this lesson you're going to learn one last technique: the muffled tone. Then you'll use it to play a fuller version of the rumba low drum part that you originally learned in Lesson 3. Once you've mastered the new part, you'll play a few variations on it.

To make the muffled tone, start with your hand in the same position above the drum as for the open tone. When you bring your hand down, the palm does not make contact with the edge of the drum as it does for the open tone. Only the fingers make contact with the drumhead. Bring them down flat, so the entire length of the fingers hits the head at the same time. Keep your thumb pulled back and out of the way. To get the fingers to hit flat you need to raise your elbow slightly:

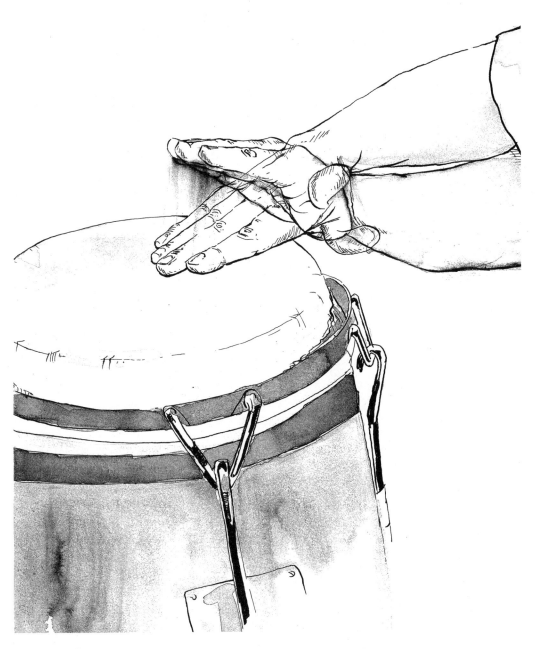

After your fingers make contact with the head, press them down to muffle the sound. If you're playing fast, you will press for just an instant. The higher you raise your elbow, the more pressure you can exert. Try applying different amounts of pressure to hear the difference it makes in the sound.

It may also help you to think of the muffled tone as a modified slap. Accelerate your fingers toward the head just

⊘
Memory Tip
The diagonal line through the symbol for the open tone reminds you to muffle the tone.

like for a slap, but keep them straight so the entire length of the fingers hits instead of just the pads of the fingertips. Then, at the first sensation in your fingers that you've made contact with the head, slam the brakes on, turning the stroke from a slap into a press. If you stop the momentum of your hand at the right instant, you can actually feel the head vibrate as you press your fingers into it. When your fingers are fully pressed into the head, the vibration stops.

Now you're ready to try the muffled tone in a fuller version of the rumba low drum part. Here's the part the way you first learned it:

Rhythm 3-1: Rumba low drum part

1	+	2	+	3	+	4	+
✳				✳		O	
L				L		R	

Here's the full part, with a touch and a muffled tone added, charted with the clave:

Rhythm 23-1: Full rumba low drum part

1	+	2	+	3	+	4	+	1	+	2	+	3	+	4	+
✳		•	⊘	✳		O		✳		•	⊘	✳		O	
L		L	R	L		R		L		L	R	L		R	

Now here are four variations. Before you start each chart, play two measures of the regular full part. Then start playing what's on the chart and continue playing what's written there over and over. By starting with two measures of the full part, the heart of each variation will fall at the start of each cycle of four measures:

Rhythm 23-2: Rumba low drum part, variation 1

1	+	2	+	3	+	4	+	1	+	2	+	3	+	4	+
✳		•	⊘	✳		○		✳		•	⊘	✳			⊘
L		L	R	L		R		L		L	R	L			L

(brackets: 3, 4)

1	+	2	+	3	+	4	+	1	+	2	+	3	+	4	+
⊘			✳			○		✳		•	⊘	✳		○	
R			R			R		L		L	R	L		R	

Start of cycle → (brackets: 1, 2)

Rhythm 23-3: Rumba low drum part, variation 2

1	+	2	+	3	+	4	+	1	+	2	+	3	+	4	+
✳		•	⊘	✳		○		✳		•	⊘	✳		⊘	⊘
L		L	R	L		R		L		L	R	L		R	L

(brackets: 3, 4)

1	+	2	+	3	+	4	+	1	+	2	+	3	+	4	+
⊘			✳			○		✳		•	⊘	✳		○	
R			R			R		L		L	R	L		R	

(brackets: 1, 2)

Rhythm 23-4: Rumba low drum part, variation 3

1	+	2	+	3	+	4	+	1	+	2	+	3	+	4	+
✳		•	⊘	✳			O	✳		•		⊘	⊘	⊘	⊘
L		L	R	L			R	L		L		R	L	R	L

(3)   (4)

1	+	2	+	3	+	4	+	1	+	2	+	3	+	4	+
⊘			✳			O		✳		•	⊘	✳		O	
R			R			R		L		L	R	L		R	

(1)   (2)

Rhythm 23-5: Rumba low drum part, variation 4

1	+	2	+	3	+	4	+	1	+	2	+	3	+	4	+
✳		•	⊘	✳			O	✳		•	⊘	✳		O	
L		L	R	L			R	L		L	R	L		R	

(3)   (4)

1	+	2	+	3	+	4	+	1	+	2	+	3	+	4	+
O			✳			O		✳		•	⊘	✳		O	
R			R			R		L		L	R	L		R	

(1)   (2)

Now that you know four variations, play whichever one you want every four or eight measures. Because the third variation with the five muffled tones is the densest, it would be a good idea to use it less often than the others. A dense part is like a rich dessert; it tastes best in small portions.

Group Playing Principle
Use dense variations and embellishments sparingly.

Lesson 24

Rumba middle drum part–tres golpes

The rumba middle drum part called tres golpes (trayss GOHL-pays) gives the rumba guaguanco its distinctive sound. It can be played in many different ways. In its most common form, its two open tones fall on the 2-side of the clave, which is how we've charted it here. Notice that the rhythm does not begin on 1:

Rhythm 24-1: Rumba tres golpes

1	+	2	+	3	+	4	+	1	+	2	+	3	+	4	+
	△	△	✳		△	✳	△	○		△	○		△	✳	△
	L	R	L		L	R	L	R		L	R		L	R	L

This is a difficult rhythm, so before you try to say the clave with it, you may first want to concentrate on learning just the hand pattern. If breaking a new pattern into pieces has been working for you, try that. Or you might try building the pattern from the ground up, starting with a few notes and adding the rest one or two at a time until you can play the rhythm all the way through. However you learn the pattern, when it feels comfortable in your hands and makes sense to your ears, add the clave.

For those of you who never get enough, you can also say a palito pattern while playing this rhythm. Here's the second palito pattern you learned as Rhythm 13-3 charted with the syllables we use to say it:

Rhythm 24-2: Palito pattern 2

1	+	2	+	3	+	4	+	1	+	2	+	3	+	4	+
CHA	KA		OO	CHA	KA		OO	CHA		CHA		CHA	KA		OO

These syllables are just a suggestion. Each teacher has a different way of saying rhythms and this is our way. We're sure you'll find a way that will work for you.

Now say the palito pattern while playing the rumba tres golpes part. In the following chart, the palito pattern is written underneath the count row:

Rhythm 24-3: Rumba tres golpes with palito pattern

1	+	2	+	3	+	4	+	1	+	2	+	3	+	4	+
X	X		X	X	X		X	X		X		X	X		X
	△	△	∗		△	∗	△	○		△	○		△	∗	△
	L	R	L		L	R	L	R		L	R		L	R	L

You can also use your voice to learn drum parts. Most cultures where rhythms are not traditionally written down assign a specific syllable to each drum stroke as a form of oral notation. Saying a rhythm frees you to concentrate on the pattern without having to think about hand technique. It also stores the pattern in a way that makes it easy to remember. If your hands ever forget what to play, your voice can sing them their part.

The rumba tres golpes can be played as a round by two drummers. In the chart below, the second drum part enters after one measure of the first drum part. The tones in the second drum part fall on the 3-side of the clave. At the end of the chart continue playing both parts:

Rhythm 24-4: Rumba tres golpes as a round

1	+	2	+	3	+	4	+	1	+	2	+	3	+	4	+
	△	△	*		△	*	△	O		△	O		△	*	△
	L	R	L		L	R	L	R		L	R		L	R	L

1	+	2	+	3	+	4	+	1	+	2	+	3	+	4	+
									△	△	*		△	*	△
									L	R	L		L	R	L

1	+	2	+	3	+	4	+	1	+	2	+	3	+	4	+
	△	△	*		△	*	△	O		△	O		△	*	△
	L	R	L		L	R	L	R		L	R		L	R	L

1	+	2	+	3	+	4	+	1	+	2	+	3	+	4	+
O		△	O		△	*	△		△	△	*		△	*	△
R		L	R		L	R	L		L	R	L		L	R	L

Lesson 25

Rumba quinto

The quinto player is a storyteller who uses the drum to weave a tale through the fabric of a rhythm. The other parts don't stop for the quinto as they do for a rock drummer's solo. The quinto part plays over the other parts and dances in the open spaces between them while they continue at full force. So the quinto player must know when to speak and when to be silent, when to say little and when to say much, when to let a rhythm simmer and when to bring it to a boil. This requires experience, skill, creativity, and an ego capable of restraint. The quinto part must always serve the whole rhythm, and not merely draw attention to the player.

**The quinto player knows
when to let a rhythm simmer
and when to bring it to a boil.**

When music and dance go together, the quinto player engages in a dialogue with the dancers, inspiring them by adding surprise and intensity to the groove while at the same time drawing inspiration from them and translating their movements into the language of the drum. So the quinto player must not only be an eloquent speaker and rapt listener, but also an intent observer.

At the deepest level, improvisation is an art that cannot be taught. It springs from some mysterious source within. But quinto playing isn't always pure improvisation, even though it may sound like it. A quinto part often has an underlying structure that serves as a foundation for improvisation. This structure is made up of a pattern of notes called marks. The marks form an internal reference rhythm for the quinto player that is different from any other pattern in the rhythm, including the clave. In this lesson, you'll learn one set of marks for a rumba quinto part that could become the basis for your own improvisation.

Here are the marks:

1	+	2	+	3	+	4	+	1	+	2	+	3	+	4	+
	X	X				X		X		X	X			X		X

Notice that the pattern is one measure long, while the clave
is two measures. This means that the pattern fits differently
with each half of the clave. Also notice that the pattern does
not have a note on 1, which gives it a suspended feel.

Start by playing the pattern with two slaps and then two
open tones, with touches added. Say the clave as you play:

Rhythm 25-1: Rumba quinto

1	+	2	+	3	+	4	+	1	+	2	+	3	+	4	+
•	△	△	•	•	○	•	○	•	△	△	•	•	○	•	○
R	L	R	L	R	L	R	L	R	L	R	L	R	L	R	L

Did you say the clave while you played? It's important.
Otherwise the pattern is likely to get turned around in your
head and the first open tone will start to feel like 1.

Since a quinto part should sound crisp and clean, you're
now going to take out the touches. You're also going to play
the second open tone with your right hand, so that the entire
hand pattern alternates between left and right:

Rhythm 25-2: Rumba quinto

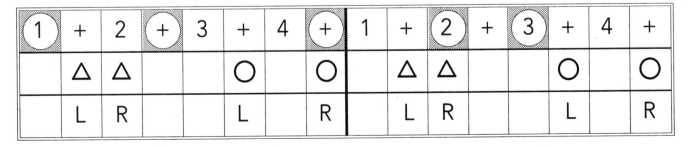

1	+	2	+	3	+	4	+	1	+	2	+	3	+	4	+
	△	△			○		○		△	△			○		○
	L	R			L		R		L	R			L		R

Now that you know a basic pattern, you can begin to vary it as a step towards improvisation. As you work through the five variations that follow, keep coming back to the basic pattern so that you get used to shifting back and forth.

The first variation has the same rhythm as the basic pattern played with different techniques. Instead of playing slap-slap-tone-tone, play slap-tone-slap-tone:

Rhythm 25-3: Rumba quinto, variation 1

1	+	2	+	3	+	4	+	1	+	2	+	3	+	4	+
	△	O			△		O		△	O			△		O
	L	R			L		R		L	R			L		R

The second variation is the same as the basic pattern, with added open tones:

Rhythm 25-4: Rumba quinto, variation 2

1	+	2	+	3	+	4	+	1	+	2	+	3	+	4	+
O	△	△			O		O		△	△			O	O	O
R	L	R			L		R		L	R			L	R	L

The third variation is straight off-beats. This pattern is the same as the basic pattern except the slap in the right hand is on the AND of 2 instead of 2 in both measures:

Rhythm 25-5: Rumba quinto, variation 3

1	+	2	+	3	+	4	+	1	+	2	+	3	+	4	+
	△		△		O		O		△		△		O		O
	L		R		L		R		L		R		L		R

The fourth variation is also straight off-beats, but this time it's pure slaps:

Rhythm 25-6: Rumba quinto, variation 4

1	+	2	+	3	+	4	+	1	+	2	+	3	+	4	+
	△		△		△		△		△		△		△		△
	L		R		L		R		L		R		L		R

To play these off-beats fast with the clave, you have to fight the magnetic pull of the on-beats. This force sneaks up on you. Get a partner to play clave for you or record yourself and play along and you'll see what we mean. After playing for a while at a quick tempo you may start thinking: "Hey! This isn't so hard!" This means that either you're a quick learner or you've stopped fighting and without realizing it have surrendered to the current of the on-beats.

The last variation alternates between the basic pattern and the straight off-beats within the span of a single clave pattern:

Rhythm 25-7: Rumba quinto, variation 5

1	+	2	+	3	+	4	+	1	+	2	+	3	+	4	+
	△	△				O		O		△		△		△		△
	L	R				L		R		L		R		L		R

Now you're ready to put all the rumba parts together with your friends. You can take turns playing quinto. When it's your turn, start with the basic pattern and begin mixing and matching it with the variations you just learned. You can change any variation by substituting open tones for slaps and vice versa, or by playing all the notes as open tones or all the notes as slaps.

Then try improvising freely. Remember that the groove played by the other players is there to support you. Keep coming back to the basic quinto pattern so your improvisation will have continuity. Think of your explorations as trips in a battery-charged car; every time you return to the basic pattern your batteries are recharged for further exploration.

You don't have to play a lot of notes to be a good quinto player. You don't have play with blinding speed. You just have to put the notes you play in the right spots. Don't be afraid of silence; it can be eloquent. When you speak, speak from the heart. Learn to say a lot in a few words. Make every note count.

9

Advanced rhythms in six

This chapter brings you deeper into the land of six. It starts with a lesson on the Afro-Cuban cowbell part that takes the place of the clave in most rhythms in six. Once you learn the bell part, you'll learn how to add it to a new three-part bembe rhythm. Then you'll get a chance to work on your muffled tones as you learn variations of a bembe middle drum part you already know.

In the middle of the chapter, you'll play various 3-beat combinations in six to give you different perspectives on the terrain. Then you'll play some variations on heel-toe patterns just as you did in four, to prepare you to improvise in six. In the last lesson, you'll venture out to an exotic province in the land of six known as the abakwa.

Lesson 26

The Afro-Cuban cowbell in six

In most Afro-Cuban rhythms in six, the cowbell pattern takes the place of the clave as the reference rhythm. It is played entirely on the neck of the bell. The pattern is two measures long in 6/8 time, where each measure contains 6 eighth notes. Clap the pattern while counting "1, 2, 3, 4, 5, 6":

Rhythm 26-1: Cowbell in six

1	2	3	4	5	6	1	2	3	4	5	6
X		X		X	X		X		X		X

To understand this bell part better, it will help you to feel the pattern with on-beats and off-beats. So just for now, try counting it in 6/4. Each measure in 6/4 has 6 quarter notes, or 12 eighth notes. So this pattern, which takes two measures in 6/8, takes only one measure in 6/4. Once you feel the on-beats and off-beats, you'll have an easier time when you go back to counting it in 6/8.

Musical Time-Out: Changing the count

Changing how you count a rhythm doesn't change how the rhythm sounds. It only changes how you perceive the rhythm internally. Here we're counting the cowbell pattern two different ways to help you get the correct feel of the rhythm.

In 6/4, the first three notes of the bell pattern are on-beats (1, 2, and 3) while the last four are off-beats (the ANDs of 3, 4, 5, and 6). This splits the pattern roughly in half. Clap or play the pattern while counting "1 AND 2 AND 3 AND 4 AND 5 AND 6 AND." Notice how different the two halves feel:

Rhythm 26-2: Cowbell in six counted in 6/4

1	+	2	+	3	+	4	+	5	+	6	+
X		X		X	X		X		X		X

You can also feel the difference between the two halves by playing the pattern in tone-touch form:

Rhythm 26-3: Cowbell in 6/4 in tone-touch form

1	+	2	+	3	+	4	+	5	+	6	+
O	•	O	•	O	O	•	O	•	O	•	O
R	L	R	L	R	L	R	L	R	L	R	L

Notice that your right hand plays the on-beats of the first
half of the pattern; then your left hand takes over and plays
the off-beats of the second half.

Now that you've had a chance to feel the cowbell pattern in
6/4, we're going to return to counting it in 6/8, the usual
time signature for rhythms in six. Although this detour into
6/4 may have seemed like a digression, the insight you've
gained into the bell pattern will pay off later when you begin
playing more complex rhythms in six.

When this cowbell pattern is played in pure form on the
drum, it's often played with slaps replacing most of the open
tones. In the following chart, only the first and last notes of
the pattern are played as open tones. All the other notes are
slaps in the right hand. Notice the drop stroke in your left
hand on 2 of the first measure. Leave your left hand on the
drumhead while you play the slaps to make them crisp:

Rhythm 26-4: Cowbell in six on the drum

1	2	3	4	5	6	1	2	3	4	5	6
O	⊖̇	△		△	△		△		△		O
R	L	R		R	R		R		R		L

If you're playing a rhythm in six and no one has a cowbell,
you can play the cowbell pattern on the drum in this way.

There are many ways to adapt the cowbell pattern for the
drum. Here's another example:

Rhythm 26-5: Cowbell in six on the drum

1	2	3	4	5	6	1	2	3	4	5	6
✳	•	O	•	△	△	•	O	•	△	•	△
R	L	R	L	R	L	R	L	R	L	R	L

Now that you're familiar with the cowbell in six, you should know that there is also a clave in six. The clave pattern is contained within the cowbell pattern and is simply the cowbell pattern without the pick-up notes on beat 5 in the first measure and beat 6 in the second measure:

Rhythm 26-6: Clave in six

1	2	3	4	5	6	1	2	3	4	5	6
X		X			X		X		X		

Occasionally you will hear someone playing the clave in six, but usually the cowbell pattern is played instead.

Now go back and say the bell pattern with all the other bembe parts you've learned. When you do this, you'll notice that although the bell pattern itself remains constant, it changes the sound and feel of every rhythm it's played with. It animates, illuminates, and drives whatever it touches. If our house were on fire and we could only take one rhythm with us, the cowbell in six would definitely be it.

**If our house were on fire
and we could only take one rhythm with us,
the cowbell in six would definitely be it.**

Lesson 27

A bembe conversation

When several drums are played by different players, the melody formed by open tones moving from drum to drum is often referred to as a conversation. In this lesson, the low, middle, and high drums carry on a conversation with each other when you combine the three parts.

You already know the middle drum part–tumbao in six–so the only new challenge will be combining it with the cowbell pattern. From now on, when we chart the cowbell pattern in six it will appear as circles around numbers in the count row, just like the clave in four:

Rhythm 7-1: Tumbao in six, middle drum

(1)	2	(3)	4	(5)	(6)	1	(2)	3	(4)	5	(6)
ᴗ	•	△	•	○	○	ᴗ	•	△	•	○	○
L	L	R	L	R	R	L	L	R	L	R	R

The high drum part is new. Notice that its open tones fall on beats 3 and 4 of each measure, while the open tones in the middle drum part fall on beats 5 and 6:

Rhythm 27-1: Bembe high drum part

(1)	2	(3)	4	(5)	(6)	1	(2)	3	(4)	5	(6)
✳	•	○	○	•	•	✳	•	○	○	•	•
R	R	L	R	R	L	R	R	L	R	R	L

The low drum part is the most challenging:

Rhythm 27-2: Bembe low drum part

(1)	2	(3)	4	(5)	(6)	1	(2)	3	(4)	5	(6)
○	ᴗ	•	△	•	△	•	ᴗ	•	△	•	△
R	L	L	R	L	R	L	L	L	R	L	R

Group Playing Principle
*Once you've mastered
your part, work on
listening to how the
other parts fit with it.*

Although each of these three drum parts is satisfying to play alone, to hear the conversation you need to hear all three parts at once. But hanging on to your own part while listening to the others is no easy feat. When you first learn a part, it takes all your concentration just to play it without making mistakes. If you give in to the temptation to listen to the other parts–especially a solo–you can quickly lose your place. Only when you've really mastered your part will you have the luxury of listening to how the other parts fit with it.

Lesson 28

Bembe middle drum part variations

In this lesson, you're going to go back to the same bembe middle drum part you worked with in Lessons 9 and 10 to build some additional variations using muffled tones. So you don't have to flip pages, here's the basic part again:

Rhythm 9-2: Bembe middle drum part

1	2	3	4	5	6
▽	•	✳	•	△	•
L	L	R	L	R	L

Since you've already learned two variations on this part, the first variation in this lesson is called variation 3. It has muffled tones on beats 1 and 2 of the pattern, and an open tone on beat 3. Insert this variation as the first of every four repetitions of the basic pattern, the same way you did with variations 1 and 2. That means you'll play variation 3 once, followed by three repetitions of Rhythm 9-2:

Rhythm 28-1: Bembe middle drum part, variation 3

1	2	3	4	5	6
⊘	⊘	◯	⊖̇	△	•
R	L	R	L	R	L

Variation 4 is the same as variation 3, except that it adds two
additional muffled tones on beats 5 and 6 of the preceding
measure. Insert this variation once in every four repetitions
of Rhythm 9-2 as you've been doing with the other
variations. Start by playing three measures of Rhythm 9-2.
On beat 5 of the fourth measure–which is where the
following chart begins–start variation 4. Then continue
with Rhythm 9-2 until the cycle repeats:

Rhythm 28-2: Bembe middle drum part, variation 4

5	6	1	2	3	4	5	6
⊘	⊘	⊘	⊘	◯	⊖̇	△	•
R	L	R	L	R	L	R	L

You may have noticed that playing this variation has the
effect of obscuring the 1. This effect is created by playing the
same stroke in a series that begins before the 1 and ends
after the 1. In variation 4, that stroke is a muffled tone. The
momentary disorientation caused by obscuring the 1 adds a
delicious tension to the rhythm.

Now put these two muffled tone variations together. Since
this chart is four measures long, there's room to chart two
repetitions of the cowbell pattern:

Rhythm 28-3: Bembe middle drum part, variations 3 and 4

1	2	3	4	5	6	1	2	3	4	5	6
⊘	⊘	○	⊖̇	△	•	⊽	•	✳	•	⊘	⊘
R	L	R	L	R	L	L	L	R	L	R	L

1	2	3	4	5	6	1	2	3	4	5	6
⊘	⊘	○	⊖̇	△	•	⊽	•	✳	•	△	•
R	L	R	L	R	L	L	L	R	L	R	L

Finally, mix and match the four variations you now know, inserting them at regular intervals as you play the basic part. Remember that this part also goes with the other bembe parts you learned in Lessons 8 and 9.

As you begin to do more group playing, you may have to adjust your style a bit. For example, some people like to close their eyes when they play. Turning inward is fine if you're playing alone in your living room, but when you're playing in a group, you should keep your eyes open to stay connected and watch for signals from others. You may get a distress signal from someone who's lost or unsolicited help from someone who's noticed that you're lost. If the group has a leader, you may get a signal to change the tempo or volume.

Group Playing Principle
Keep your eyes open.

You may also be used to stopping whenever you make a mistake or get lost. But when you play in a group, you've got to keep going no matter what. When you make a mistake, ignore it and move on. When you get lost, listen and jump back in as soon as possible. If you totally choke and can't remember your part at all, at least keep going mentally with the rhythm until something comes to you. The rhythm is a train that is going to keep moving with or without you. If you can't jump back on, at least run alongside.

Group Playing Principle
Keep going.

Lesson 29

3-Beat combination exercises

So far in this chapter, we've presented a lot of new rhythms in six. To give you a chance to digest those rhythms and integrate them better, we're going to do something different here. The exercises that follow are designed to both work your technique and deepen your felt sense of the structure of rhythms in six and their relationship to the cowbell. In these exercises, you're going to take 3-beat sections made up of one open tone and two slaps and arrange the three strokes in different ways.

Here's the first exercise: tone-slap-slap. It looks simple but it's a little tricky to play because each 3-beat section starts with a different hand:

Rhythm 29-1: Tone-slap-slap

1	2	3	4	5	6
◯	△	△	◯	△	△
R	L	R	L	R	L

Once you can play the rhythm correctly, shift your focus to technique. Close your eyes and listen to yourself play. The tones should be clear and the slaps crisp, even when you play fast. And your slaps should sound exactly the same in both hands. If there's a difference, analyze what your strong hand is doing and mimic it in the other hand. Let your strong hand teach your weak hand how to play.

Practice Principle
Let your strong hand teach your weak hand how to play.

Now say the cowbell pattern while you play:

Rhythm 29-2: Tone-slap-slap

①	2	③	4	⑤	⑥	1	②	3	④	5	⑥
◯	△	△	◯	△	△	◯	△	△	◯	△	△
R	L	R	L	R	L	R	L	R	L	R	L

Next switch the open tone from being the first note of every 3-beat section to being the last. Keep saying the cowbell while you play so you don't lose track of 1:

Rhythm 29-3: Slap-slap-tone

①	2	③	4	⑤	⑥	1	②	3	④	5	⑥
△	△	◯	△	△	◯	△	△	◯	△	△	◯
R	L	R	L	R	L	R	L	R	L	R	L

Do the same thing again, only this time make the open tone the middle note of every 3-beat section:

Rhythm 29-4: Slap-tone-slap

①	2	③	4	⑤	⑥	1	②	3	④	5	⑥
△	◯	△	△	◯	△	△	◯	△	△	◯	△
R	L	R	L	R	L	R	L	R	L	R	L

Now that you've heard and felt each combination with the cowbell, you're going to put two combinations together and play them one after the other. In the first two measures, the open tone comes first; in the second two it comes last. Notice that when you make the transition from the first combination to the second, you play four slaps in a row. Also notice that when you finish the second combination and make the transition back to the first, you play two open tones in a row. These transitions serve as landmarks for the ears, eyes, and hands. Use them to stay on course.

This combined rhythm is challenging to play. Take a break from saying the cowbell while you learn it, so you can concentrate on mastering the hand pattern. You can add the cowbell later:

Rhythm 29-5: Combination exercise

1	2	3	4	5	6	1	2	3	4	5	6
O	△	△	O	△	△	O	△	△	O	△	△
R	L	R	L	R	L	R	L	R	L	R	L

1	2	3	4	5	6	1	2	3	4	5	6
△	△	O	△	△	O	△	△	O	△	△	O
R	L	R	L	R	L	R	L	R	L	R	L

Since these exercises work your technique, it would be a good idea for you to check in now on how you're doing. One way to do this is to watch yourself play in the mirror. While you're playing, check your posture and look for areas of tension. Are your shoulders relaxed? How about your jaw? Are your wrists and hands loose? Notice how close your hands are to the head. Are your movements efficient and symmetrical? You never outgrow your need to work on technique. Keep asking yourself: What could be lighter, freer, easier?

Practice Principle
Practice in the mirror occasionally to check your posture and technique.

**Keep asking yourself:
What could be lighter, freer, easier?**

Lesson 30

Heel-toe patterns in six

If you worked through the chapter on heel-toe patterns, you've already mastered the hand techniques used in this lesson. What's new here is the count. You're going to shift from counting the heel-toe patterns in four to counting them in six. Then you're going to substitute tones and slaps for heels and toes to create variations just as you did in four.

You're going to start by extending the heel-toe-toe-heel pattern to cover two measures of six beats each. This is the length of one repetition of the cowbell part in six. Count out loud as you play: "1, 2, 3, 4, 5, 6." This will solidify the cycle for you and make sure you're feeling the six. The pattern begins with the right heel just as it did in four. But notice that the second measure begins with the right toe:

Rhythm 30-1: Heel-toe-toe-heel pattern in six

1	2	3	4	5	6	1	2	3	4	5	6
▽	•	•	▽	▽	•	•	▽	▽	•	•	▽
R	L	R	L	R	L	R	L	R	L	R	L

Try saying the cowbell pattern while you play to make sure you understand how it fits with this heel-toe pattern.

Now you're going to build a couple musical phrases, just as you did with the heel-toe patterns in four. For the first variation, put open tones on the first beat of the first measure and the second beat of the second measure:

Rhythm 30-2: Heel-toe-toe-heel pattern in six, variation 1

1	2	3	4	5	6	1	2	3	4	5	6
◯	•	•	⌣	⌣	•	•	◯	⌣	•	•	⌣
R	L	R	L	R	L	R	L	R	L	R	L

Next, add a slap after each open tone:

Rhythm 30-3: Heel-toe-toe-heel pattern in six, variation 2

1	2	3	4	5	6	1	2	3	4	5	6
◯	•	△	⌣	⌣	•	•	◯	⌣	△	•	⌣
R	L	R	L	R	L	R	L	R	L	R	L

Now switch to the heel-heel-toe-toe pattern:

Rhythm 30-4: Heel-heel-toe-toe pattern in six

1	2	3	4	5	6	1	2	3	4	5	6
⌣	⌣	•	•	⌣	⌣	•	•	⌣	⌣	•	•
R	L	R	L	R	L	R	L	R	L	R	L

As your first variation on this pattern, add an open tone and slap in each hand:

Rhythm 30-5 : Heel-heel-toe-toe pattern in six, variation 1

1	2	3	4	5	6	1	2	3	4	5	6
◯	⌒	△	•	⌒	◯	•	△	⌒	⌒	•	•
R	L	R	L	R	L	R	L	R	L	R	L

This last variation includes some muffled tones:

Rhythm 30-6: Heel-heel-toe-toe pattern in six, variation 2

1	2	3	4	5	6	1	2	3	4	5	6
◯	⌒	△	•	⌒	◯	•	△	⊘	⊘	⊘	⊘
R	L	R	L	R	L	R	L	R	L	R	L

Playing Principle
Play rhythms for a long time.

It's your turn now. Go ahead and make up your own substitutions. If you find one that works and feels good, try playing it for a long time. A rhythm played for an hour is different from the same rhythm played for a minute, just as running five miles is different from running a hundred yards. It takes a while for the body to settle in and become attuned to a rhythm. Give yourself time. You'll never experience the magic of losing yourself to a rhythm if you quit too soon. There's no shortcut to bliss.

Something even more mystical happens when a group gets into a groove together. This usually happens only after the group has been playing a rhythm for a long time. When everyone's sense of time becomes synchronized, the rhythm locks. At that point, real time is overthrown. A sense of unity takes over, a feeling of transcendence, of being one with something larger than yourself. Once you've been there, you can't wait to get back.

Lesson 31

The abakwa

The abakwa pattern gets its name from the secret male society in Cuba that uses it as a foundation for rhythms in six. The pattern is traditionally played with sticks on a wood block or the side of a drum, but it can also be adapted for the conga drum, which is how you're going to play it.

The pattern divides two measures of 6 beats into three 4-beat sections. In the basic abakwa pattern, each 4-beat section has the pattern "ON-ON-ON-off." Notice that every fourth beat is silent. Clap the rhythm while counting "1, 2, 3, 4, 5, 6":

Rhythm 31-1: The abakwa

1	2	3	4	5	6	1	2	3	4	5	6
X	X	X		X	X	X		X	X	X	

The abakwa pattern is unlike any of the bembe rhythms you've learned, which can be divided into 3-beat or 6-beat sections. It's also unlike the cowbell pattern in six, which is a single 12-beat phrase. The abakwa gets its distinct feel from its unique structure of three 4-beat sections. This difference in structure creates the rhythmic tug you'll feel when you play the abakwa against other rhythms in six.

The bembe abakwa rhythm that follows is like the basic abakwa pattern because it also divides 12 beats into three 4-beat sections. But unlike that pattern, which has an empty fourth beat in each 4-beat section, this rhythm has an empty second beat in each section:

Rhythm 31-2: Bembe abakwa rhythm, high drum part

1	2	3	4	5	6	1	2	3	4	5	6
O		⌣	•	O		⌣	•	O		⌣	•
R		L	L	R		L	L	R		L	L

To feel the tug of this abakwa rhythm, you need to play it against other rhythms in six. It can be played with any other bembe rhythms you know, but it goes especially well with the two drum parts that follow. Here's the part for the low drum:

Rhythm 31-3: Bembe low drum part

1	2	3	4	5	6	1	2	3	4	5	6
O		✳	✳	✳		O	✳		✳	✳	
R		L	R	L		R	L		R	L	

The part for the middle drum has two variations. Here's the first variation:

Rhythm 31-4: Bembe middle drum part, variation 1

1	2	3	4	5	6	1	2	3	4	5	6
✳	△		✳	✳	✳	✳	△	✳	O		
L	R		R	L	R	L	R	L	R		

In the second variation, an empty beat is inserted on 3 of the second measure:

Rhythm 31-5: Bembe middle drum part, variation 2

1	2	3	4	5	6	1	2	3	4	5	6
✳	△		✳	✳	✳	✳	△		✳	○	
L	R		R	L	R	L	R		L	R	

Here's another bembe rhythm with three parts in which one of the parts has a structure like the abakwa. The high drum part divides 12 beats into three 4-beat sections; the first two sections are identical, while the third section has two open tones:

Rhythm 31-6: Bembe abakwa rhythm, high drum part

1	2	3	4	5	6	1	2	3	4	5	6
⌣	•	△	•	⌣	•	△	•	○	○	△	•
L	L	R	L	L	L	R	L	R	R	R	L

The middle drum part tracks the cowbell pattern, with an open tone on the second note. Feel free to insert timekeeping touches in the left hand between the right hand strokes to keep the rhythm steady:

Rhythm 31-7: Bembe middle drum part

1	2	3	4	5	6	1	2	3	4	5	6
△		○		△	△		△		△		△
R		R		R	R		R		R		R

The low drum part has two open tones that emphasize two notes of the cowbell pattern. It gives your left hand a good workout:

Rhythm 31-8: Bembe low drum part

1	2	3	4	5	6	1	2	3	4	5	6
⌣	•	⌣	•	O	O	⌣	•	△	•	⌣	•
L	L	L	L	R	R	L	L	R	L	L	L

Now try to find two other drummers–and a cowbell player–and play each set of these three-part bembe rhythms together.

10

Playing on two drums

If you're thinking of skipping this chapter just because you don't have another drum–don't. Although we show you how to play rhythms on two drums, you can easily play them on one. Two-drum rhythms are often adapted for one drum by playing open tones meant for the second drum as bass tones on the single drum. This method works well for the two-drum versions of tumbao, songo, and rumba presented in this chapter. For the two-drum bembe rhythms, you can play the part meant for the second drum with your right hand on the side of the drum.

When you play on two drums, they should be tuned to different pitches. The difference in pitch makes melody possible. When we talk about two-drum rhythms, we'll refer to the higher-pitched drum as the high drum, and the lower-pitched drum as the low drum. But these can be any two drums tuned to different pitches: a tumba and a conga, a conga and quinto, or a tumba and a quinto.

A common tuning is to have the high drum tuned a fourth higher than the low drum. That means if you think of the low drum as "DO," the high drum would be tuned to "FA." Many drummers use different tunings, however, and you can use whatever sounds good to you.

The low drum is usually placed to the right of the high drum for right-handed drummers (and to the left for left-handed drummers). It's also placed slightly ahead of the high drum, to leave room for the right leg.

Many drummers tilt the high drum toward the low drum–instead of straight forward–to make it easy for the right hand to move between the two drums.

***Playing Principle**
Adapt two-drum rhythms to a single drum by playing open tones intended for the second drum as bass tones on the single drum.*

Tilting a drum will usually raise its pitch a half step. So if you're trying to get two drums in tune with each other, you have to tune each drum in the position you plan to play it in. This means tuning the low drum while it's standing flat on the floor and tuning the high drum while it's tilted.

Lesson 32

Tumbao and songo

Tumbao can be played several ways on two drums. The first version here begins with a measure of the one-drum tumbao in four you already know. In the second measure, you add a single open tone on the second drum. It falls on the AND of 3.

Memory Tip
The second circle indicates an open tone on the second drum.

To add this open tone you need to change your hand pattern slightly. Because your right hand needs to be on the second drum on the AND of 3 in the second measure, you have to play the open tone on 4 on the first drum in the left hand. This gives your right hand time to move back to the first drum to play the open tone on the AND of 4:

Rhythm 32-1: Tumbao on two drums

1	+	2	+	3	+	4	+	1	+	2	+	3	+	4	+
▽	•	△	•	◡	•	○	○	▽	•	△	•	▽	◎	○	○
L	L	R	L	L	L	R	R	L	L	R	L	L	R	L	R

Remember, if you're playing this on one drum, play the open tone intended for the second drum as a bass tone in the right hand.

The next version of tumbao is the one you'll be combining with other rhythms in this chapter. This version has two open tones on the low drum. They can be played on either the 3-side or the 2-side of the clave. In this chapter, you're going to be playing them on the 3-side of the son clave, which is the first measure in this chart:

Rhythm 32-2: Tumbao on two drums

1	+	2	+	3	+	4	+	1	+	2	+	3	+	4	+
⌣	•	△	◎	◎	⊖	○	○	⌣	•	△	•	⌣	•	○	○
L	L	R	R	R	L	R	R	L	L	R	L	L	L	R	R

Notice that the right hand plays the two open tones on the low drum immediately after a right hand slap. That means you have to move the right hand quickly to the low drum to stay on the beat. Also notice the drop stroke in the left hand on the AND of 3 in the first measure. The left hand drops lightly and then rises immediately so the open tones that follow won't be muffled.

The next rhythm is songo. Songo is a relatively new rhythm that was popularized by the Cuban group Los Van Van in the 1970s and 1980s. The second half of songo resembles tumbao, but the rhythm starts quite differently. When songo starts on the 3-side of the clave, it starts not on 1, but on the AND of 1. The first three notes are all off-beats played in the left hand.

To make songo easier to learn, we've broken it in half. Start with the first half, counting "1 AND 2 AND 3 AND 4 AND" as you play. Notice that we've charted songo with the rumba clave:

Rhythm 32-3: Songo (1st half)

1	+	2	+	3	+	4	+
	○		✳		△	◎	◎
	L		L		L	R	R

Now play the second half. Notice its resemblance to tumbao:

Rhythm 32-4: Songo (2nd half)

1	+	2	+	3	+	4	+
ᗑ	•	△	•	○	○	◎	◎
L	L	R	L	R	L	R	R

Finally, put the two halves together:

Rhythm 32-5: Songo

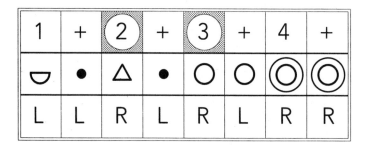

Lesson 33

Tumbao to songo and back

Tumbao, songo, and rumba are cousins in the same family of rhythms. So by using transitions, it's possible to move seamlessly from one to another. Learning how to do this will deepen your understanding of all three rhythms and their relationships. It will also allow you to create your own compositions when you play alone.

The transition from tumbao to songo occurs in the middle of tumbao, the second measure of the following chart. In the transitional measure, there are no notes on the ANDs of 1 and 2. This change from the normal pattern of tumbao creates a clean break between the two rhythms. The third and fourth measures of the chart are the normal songo.

Start by playing tumbao. When you're ready to make the transition, play the following chart. When you get to the end of the chart, continue playing songo. We've charted both rhythms with the son clave for continuity. Songo–like many Afro-Cuban rhythms–can be played with either the son or rumba clave:

Playing Principle
Many Afro-Cuban rhythms in four are played with either the son or the rumba clave.

Rhythm 33-1: Tumbao to songo

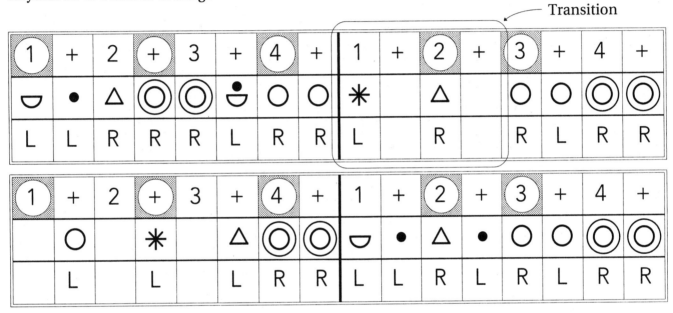

Now you're ready to learn the transition from songo to tumbao. It occurs after songo is completed and only involves the first two notes of tumbao. In the following chart, the first two measures are songo. The transition occurs at the start of the third measure. In that measure, there is no note on 1 and there is an additional slap on the AND of 1. After this clean break, you're into tumbao, which continues from there in its normal pattern.

Start by playing songo. When you're ready to make the transition, play the following chart. When you get to the end of the chart, continue playing tumbao:

Rhythm 33-2: Songo to tumbao

1	+	2	+	3	+	4	+	1	+	2	+	3	+	4	+
	○		✳		△	◎	◎	⊽	•	△	•	○	○	◎	◎
	L		L		L	R	R	L	L	R	L	R	L	R	R

1	+	2	+	3	+	4	+	1	+	2	+	3	+	4	+
	△		△	◎	◎	⊡	○	○	⊽	•	△	•	⊽	•	○	○
	L	R	R	R	L	R	R	L	L	R	L	L	L	R	R

— Transition

Now that you know how to move back and forth between tumbao and songo, alternate between the two rhythms. Pay careful attention to the clave to make sure that the transitions haven't thrown you off. If you've got a drum machine, program the clave and play along. If you've got a tape recorder, tape the clave and play along. After a while, you'll begin to hear the clave as part of the song and it will start to play internally.

Lesson 34

Rumba tres golpes

You already know the rumba tres golpes part on one drum. In this lesson, you're going to play it on two drums. On the second drum you'll be playing the two open tones from the rumba low drum part. In this way, a single drummer can approximate the sound made by two drummers and can play the full melody that is the essence of the rumba guaguanco. After you learn the basic two-drum part, you'll learn variations on it.

All you need to do to play the two-drum tres golpes part is replace the two bass tones in the one-drum part with two open tones on the low drum. The replacements occur on beat 4 of the first measure and beat 4 of the second measure. Notice that the hand pattern stays the same except that the right hand now reaches to the side for open tones on the low drum instead of forward for bass tones on a single drum:

Rhythm 34-1: Rumba tres golpes

1	+	2	+	3	+	4	+	1	+	2	+	3	+	4	+
	△	△	✳		△	◎	△	○		△	○		△	◎	△
	L	R	L		L	R	L	R		L	R		L	R	L

In this rhythm, the best way to get the relationship between the melody of the open tones and the clave into your body is to sing the tones while clapping the clave. This is a little tricky because none of the tones coincide with any of the notes of the clave. Imitate the sound of two drums by singing low and high tones:

Rhythm 34-2: Rumba tres golpes open tones

1	+	2	+	3	+	4	+	1	+	2	+	3	+	4	+
						LO	HI			HI			LO		

Now that you know exactly how this rhythm fits with the clave, you're ready for a few variations. Alternate between the basic part and each variation. The first variation adds an extra open tone on the high drum on beat 3 of the second measure and omits the slap on the AND of 3 that follows:

Rhythm 34-3: Rumba tres golpes, variation 1

1	+	2	+	3	+	4	+	1	+	2	+	3	+	4	+
	△	△	✳		△	◎	△	O		△	O	O		◎	△
	L	R	L		L	R	L	R		L	R	L		R	L

The second variation changes the first measure. It now has three slaps in a row and an extra open tone on the low drum:

Rhythm 34-4: Rumba tres golpes, variation 2

1	+	2	+	3	+	4	+	1	+	2	+	3	+	4	+
	△	△	△	◎		◎	△	O		△	O		△	◎	△
	L	R	L	R		R	L	R		L	R		L	R	L

Memory Tip
The symbol for the muffled tone on the second drum is the symbol for a muffled tone within a second circle.

The third variation brings a piece of songo into the rumba in slightly modified form. Notice that you play five off-beats in a row, starting on the AND of 3 in the second measure. The first two of those off-beats are muffled tones on the low drum. Also notice that the note on the AND of 1 in the third measure, which is an open tone in songo, is a muffled tone here:

Rhythm 34-5: Rumba tres golpes, variation 3

①	+	2	⊕	3	+	4	⊕	1	+	②	+	③	+	4	+
	△	△	✳		△	◎	△	○		△	○		⊘		⊘
	L	R	L		L	R	L	R		L	R		R		R

①	+	2	⊕	3	+	4	⊕	1	+	②	+	③	+	4	+
	⊘		✳		△	◎	△	○		△	○		△	◎	△
	L		L		L	R	L	R		L	R		L	R	L

Even though this third variation contains only a piece of songo, it contains the transitions from rumba to songo and back again. If you were playing the full songo rhythm, the transition to rumba would occur just like the transition from the piece of songo back to rumba on beat 4 of the third measure. To go from rumba to songo, just continue with songo from beat 4 of the third measure instead of returning to rumba. So now you can switch from rumba to songo and back whenever you want. In the next lesson, you'll also learn how to add tumbao to this circle of rhythms.

Lesson 35

Integrating tumbao, songo, and rumba

You already know how to get from tumbao to songo and back. You also know the transitions from rumba to songo and back. Once you learn how to get from rumba to tumbao and back, you'll be able to freely move between all three rhythms.

Here's the transition from rumba to tumbao. Notice that again for continuity we've used the son clave for both rhythms:

Rhythm 35-1: Rumba to tumbao

1	+	2	+	3	+	4	+	1	+	2	+	3	+	4	+
	△	△	✳		△	◎	△	O		△	O		△	◎	△
	L	R	L		L	R	L	R		L	R		L	R	L

1	+	2	+	3	+	4	+	1	+	2	+	3	+	4	+
	△	△	◎	◎	◒	O	O	◡	•	△	•	◡	•	O	O
	L	R	R	R	L	R	R	L	L	R	L	L	L	R	R

— Transition

Here's the transition from tumbao to rumba:

Rhythm 35-2: Tumbao to rumba

Transition —

1	+	2	+	3	+	4	+	1	+	2	+	3	+	4	+
◡	•	△	◎	◎	◒	O	O	◡	•	△	•	◡	•	◎	△
L	L	R	R	R	L	R	R	L	L	R	L	L	L	R	L

1	+	2	+	3	+	4	+	1	+	2	+	3	+	4	+
	△	△	✳		△	◎	△	O		△	O		△	◎	△
	L	R	L		L	R	L	R		L	R		L	R	L

The transition from rumba to tumbao is similar to the transition from songo to tumbao. The two slaps that took you from songo into tumbao are already a part of rumba. They fall on the AND of 1 and beat 2. All you have to do then to make the shift from rumba to tumbao is to continue with tumbao after playing those two slaps. When you get to the end of the chart for Rhythm 35-1, continue playing tumbao.

In Rhythm 35-2, the transition from tumbao back to rumba occurs on beat 4 of the second measure. Instead of playing the first of the two tones in tumbao, the right hand plays a tone on the low drum. This tone is the last tone in the rumba melody, and rumba continues from there. When you get to the end of the chart, continue playing rumba.

Finally, here's a two-bar rhythm that combines elements of all three rhythms. It starts with a piece of songo, moves to a piece of rumba, and then finishes with a piece of tumbao:

Rhythm 35-3: Combination rhythm

1	+	2	+	3	+	4	+	1	+	2	+	3	+	4	+
	O		✳		△	◎	△	O	☉	△	•	◡	•	O	O
	L		L		L	R	L	R	L	R	L	L	L	R	R

Now that you know how to move between tumbao, songo, and rumba, create your own compositions by putting them all together.

If you've come this far, we know you've been working very hard. So have we. We could all use a break. So we want to leave the world of seriousity and take a moment to tell you just what it's been like to type the word "rythym" incorrectly 995 times out of the 1000 times it appears in this book. See, it happened again.

Now wait, stay with us. There is a connection here. It might not seem obvious at first, but typing the word "rhythm" on a computer is a lot like playing a challenging rhythm on the

drum. First you have to remember the strokes. Quickly
now–you try it. Close your eyes and tell us: How many "h's"
are there and where do they go? Even if you can spell it, try
playing it on the keyboard. The right index finger has to pull
off some really fancy moves, going from the first "h" on beat
2 to the "y" on beat 3 with no stroke in between, and then
from the second "h" on beat 5 down to the "m" on beat 6
without a break. And once you add the bell pattern, the
word can really get turned around in your head.

We should have listened to our own advice: practice every
"rhythm" slowly at first; learn difficult "rhythms" a piece at a
time; etc. But no. We had to start typing at full speed and
we paid the price.

OK, back to work.

Lesson 36

Tone-slap bembe–part 1

The bembe rhythms in this lesson and the next are built
around a steady tone-slap pattern in the right hand played
on the high drum. If you don't have two drums, play the
right hand on the side of the single drum. Over the
right-hand pattern, the left hand plays a variety of rhythms
on the low drum. The low drum should be placed to the left
of the high drum, but it's up to you which drum you want
directly in front of you.

The easiest way to chart these rhythms is to eliminate the
row indicating which hand is playing, and instead use a
separate row for each hand. Putting a symbol inside
another circle works fine in a rhythm where there's only an
occasional stroke on the second drum, but where the strokes
are divided evenly between two drums, having a separate
row for each hand works better. In the following charts, the
row for the right hand is the bottom row and the row for the
left hand is the one above it.

Here's the tone-slap pattern in the right hand that will
remain constant in all the rhythms:

Rhythm 36-1: Right hand tone-slap

1	2	3	4	5	6	1	2	3	4	5	6
○	△		○	△		○	△		○	△	

This rhythmic pattern is the same as Rhythm 8-2, 8-3, and
8-4. All that's different here is that you're playing it with just
the right hand.

This right-hand pattern requires good slap technique.
Because the slap follows immediately after the open tone,
you must be efficient in your hand motions. Remember to
use a relaxed hand rather than sheer force to produce the
slap.

The first left-hand pattern answers the right hand by filling
in the beats the right hand leaves open:

Rhythm 36-2: Left-hand pattern 1

1	2	3	4	5	6	1	2	3	4	5	6
		△			○			△			○
○	△		○	△		○	△		○	△	

Now reverse the left-hand pattern and play the open tone on
beat 3 and the slap on beat 6:

Rhythm 36-3: Left-hand pattern 2

1	2	3	4	5	6	1	2	3	4	5	6
		○			△			○			△
○	△		○	△		○	△		○	△	

The next left-hand pattern is only slightly different from the last one. The open tone is still on beat 3, but the slap is now on beat 5, a beat earlier than last time. This means that you'll be playing a slap in both hands at once:

Rhythm 36-4: Left-hand pattern 3

1	2	3	4	5	6	1	2	3	4	5	6
		○		△				○		△	
○	△		○	△		○	△		○	△	

Now combine pattern 2 with pattern 3:

Rhythm 36-5: Left-hand patterns 2 and 3

1	2	3	4	5	6	1	2	3	4	5	6
		○			△			○			△
○	△		○	△		○	△		○	△	

As you learn any of these new rhythms, you'll find yourself passing through predictable stages toward mastery: first, you won't be able to play the part even *with* conscious effort; then you'll be able to play the part but *only with* conscious effort; finally, you'll be able to play the part *without* conscious effort. Often you'll discover by accident that you've reached the third stage when you look down and find your hands performing a complicated pattern without you.

At this point, the playing instructions have been transferred from your conscious mind to your body. In fact, after you've gotten used to playing a part without needing to think about it, it's often difficult to go back to consciously playing it. This is why experienced players sometimes have trouble slowing a part down to explain it to a student.

Once you can play a part unconsciously, you get to choose what you do with your conscious mind. You can focus on turning the notes into music, you can tune in to the spirit side of drumming, or you can relax and just feel the rhythm. If you're playing in a group, you can also begin to experience how all the parts fit together and open up to a sense of community with everyone around you.

Lesson 37

Tone-slap bembe–part 2

Now you're ready for the next challenge on the path to independence: playing two distinct rhythms on two drums at the same time. You've already felt the pleasure of two rhythms moving through your body at once if you've been saying the clave while learning each new drum part. In this lesson, you'll start to feel a different rhythm in each hand. While your hands are becoming more independent, your brain is becoming more integrated. As you sever the ties that bind your right and left hand, you're building the connections between your right and left brain.

For the following rhythms, the left hand is still on the low drum and the right is still on the high drum. In the charts, the left hand is still charted above the right hand.

**As you sever the ties that bind your
right and left hand, you're building the connections
between your right and left brain.**

In the first pattern, there's an open tone in the left hand on beat 5, at the same time that the right hand plays a slap. This is the first time you've played two different techniques at once:

Rhythm 37-1: Left-hand pattern 4

1	2	3	4	5	6	1	2	3	4	5	6
		△		O	O		△			O	O
O	△		O	△		O	△		O	△	

Now combine pattern 4 with pattern 3 from the last lesson and alternate between them:

Rhythm 37-2: Left-hand patterns 3 and 4

1	2	3	4	5	6	1	2	3	4	5	6
		△		O	O		O		△		
O	△		O	△		O	△		O	△	

The next left-hand figure is a slight modification of pattern 4. An open tone is added on beat 4 so you play three open tones in a row. You have to move fast from the slap to get to the first of the open tones in time:

Rhythm 37-3: Left-hand pattern 5

1	2	3	4	5	6	1	2	3	4	5	6
		△	O	O	O				△	O	O
O	△		O	△		O	△		O	△	

Now combine pattern 4 with pattern 5 and alternate
between them:

Rhythm 37-4: Left-hand patterns 4 and 5

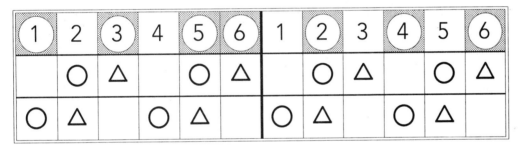

The next one is really fun because it feels like a wave going
through your body. Both hands play the same thing, but the
pattern is staggered:

Rhythm 37-5: Left-hand pattern 6

You now have a lot of left-hand patterns to play with. Here's
what we recommend you do with them. First, turn on the
answering machine. Next get your drums, light a candle,
and turn off the lights. Then settle in and get your right
hand rocking: tone-slap, tone-slap, tone-slap, tone-slap. It's
like the band warming up the audience before the lead
singer steps on stage. Take your time; don't start playing
with your left hand right away. Let the tension build for a
while. Finally, when the right hand really has the groove
flowing, and the crowd is starting to stamp their feet, allow
the left hand to make its entrance, starting with just a few
scattered strokes and then gradually increasing in intensity.
For a real thrill, start saying the cowbell pattern on top of
both rhythms.

Of course, it's not for everybody.

11

Interweaving four and six

Until now, four and six have been treated as if they existed in parallel worlds, traveling through time without ever meeting. You've tasted them separately, getting to know the unique flavor and texture of each. Now you're going to discover the pleasure of combining them. Each is great alone, like peanut butter and chocolate, but something magical happens when you experience both in a single bite.

In this chapter and the next, working with rhythms you already know, you're going to explore the interconnectedness of four and six. Playing four and six together creates what is often called a "polyrhythm." But don't be intimidated. "Polyrhythm" is just an imprecise term for any combination of two or more rhythms played at the same time. This is nothing new for you. For the last five chapters you've been saying the clave while playing the drum, so you're no stranger to polyrhythms. You're ready. Besides, the four has been in the six all along. When you bring it out, the four pushes the six like a gorilla pushing a swing.

Lesson 38

Four against six

In this lesson, you're going to divide 12 beats into 4 sections of 3 beats each. The four inside the six emerges when you play the first beat of each of those 3-beat sections.

**The four pushes the six
like a gorilla pushing a swing.**

To feel this four, in the next rhythm clap the first beat of
each of those sections while counting every beat of the six:

Rhythm 38-1: Four against six

1	2	3	4	5	6	1	2	3	4	5	6
X			X			X			X		

Notice that what we're calling six is actually two measures of
6 beats (the length of one cowbell pattern), for a total of 12.

The combination of your clapping and counting creates the
polyrhythm called "four against six." "Four against six,"
"three against four"–often the names of polyrhythms sound
like descriptions of bar-room brawls. But this is the
terminology commonly used to describe two different
rhythms played together.

**"Four against six," "three against four"–
often the names of polyrhythms
sound like descriptions of bar-room brawls.**

The same 12 beats you counted in the last rhythm can also
be counted as one measure of 6 numbered beats, with each
beat divided in half. Clap the four and count "1 AND 2 AND
3 AND 4 AND 5 AND 6 AND":

Rhythm 38-2: Four against six

1	+	2	+	3	+	4	+	5	+	6	+
X			X			X			X		

These same 12 beats can also be counted with just 4
numbered beats, with each beat divided in three.

Clap the four and count "1 AND UH 2 AND UH 3 AND UH 4 AND UH":

Rhythm 38-3: Four against six

1	+	a	2	+	a	3	+	a	4	+	a
X			X			X			X		

Group Playing Principle
Rhythms in six often start by someone counting off the four inside the six.

When someone starts a rhythm in six by counting "1, 2, 3, 4," it's these four beats inside the six that are being counted.

When the different ways of counting are stacked on top of each other, you can see that changing the count doesn't change the rhythm:

Rhythm 38-4: Four against six

1	2	3	4	5	6	1	2	3	4	5	6
1	+	2	+	3	+	4	+	5	+	6	+
1	+	a	2	+	a	3	+	a	4	+	a
X			X			X			X		

All these different ways of counting the same rhythm can be confusing. As you gain experience, you'll find that sometimes one way of counting works better than another. To keep things as simple as possible here, we're going to continue counting the 12 beats of rhythms in six as two measures of 6 beats each. We only use a different count when it makes understanding a rhythm easier for you.

Now you're going to play four against six on the drum. Play the four in the left hand and the six in the right. Use muffled tones in both hands. In the following chart, the right hand is in the bottom row:

Rhythm 38-5: Four against six

1	2	3	4	5	6	1	2	3	4	5	6
⊘			⊘			⊘			⊘		
⊘		⊘		⊘		⊘		⊘		⊘	

Listen to the combined rhythm. Let your hands teach your ears.

Now that you've heard the combined rhythm, try listening to each rhythm individually while playing both. First focus on the six in your right hand; then shift your attention to the four in your left. Bring out the six by making your right hand loud and your left hand soft; then do the reverse and bring out the four. Then move your right hand to the side of your drum while your left hand stays on the head. Then do the reverse.

As you can tell from playing four against six in different ways, many factors determine how strongly you feel the four in the six. In the next bembe rhythm, the four is emphasized because it's played as bass tones in the left hand on beats 1 and 4 of both measures:

Rhythm 38-6: Bembe rhythm

1	2	3	4	5	6	1	2	3	4	5	6
✳	•	•	✳	○	○	✳	•	•	✳	○	○
L	L	R	L	R	R	L	L	R	L	R	R

Changing what's going on around that four can change how strongly you feel it. For example, the four can be diluted by substituting a bass tone for the touch in the right hand on beat 3 of each measure:

Rhythm 38-7: Bembe rhythm, variation

①	2	③	4	⑤	⑥	1	②	3	④	5	⑥
✳	•	✳	✳	◯	◯	✳	•	✳	✳	◯	◯
L	L	R	L	R	R	L	L	R	L	R	R

The heavier you play the bass tone on 3 in relation to the bass tone on 4, the stronger the six feel is.

Now you're going to learn the four against the cowbell pattern in six, a combination found in many Afro-Cuban rhythms. Start with the four in your left hand and the cowbell pattern in your right:

Rhythm 38-8: Four against the cowbell pattern in six

1	2	3	4	5	6	1	2	3	4	5	6
⊘			⊘			⊘			⊘		
⊘		⊘		⊘	⊘		⊘		⊘		⊘

Notice that there are only two places where the right and left hands play notes at the same time: on the first and last notes of the four. Use these two meeting places as reference points to make sure that the four and the six are lined up properly. When they are, the combined rhythm really trucks along.

Practice Principle
You don't need a drum to practice polyrhythms.

Polyrhythms like these are perfect for practicing when you can't play a drum. Because you're learning pure rhythm rather than technique, you can practice them on anything: a tabletop, a book, the dashboard.

You can also play a rhythm on your thighs, or get two distinct tones by playing with one hand on your thigh and one on your chest. Playing a rhythm directly on your body is quiet, it's easy on the hands, and–most important–it drives the rhythm deep into the cells. When you play a rhythm on your own flesh, you become both musician and instrument. Your rhythmic life doesn't have to stop at ten just because that's when your neighbors go to sleep.

The body can also be used for teaching a rhythm to someone else. Sometimes our brains distort what our eyes and ears perceive. That's why you will often see a teacher play a rhythm directly on a student's back. What confuses the eye and ear can often be understood directly by the body.

Practice Principle
Play rhythms on your body.

**Your rhythmic life doesn't have to stop at ten
just because that's when your neighbors go to sleep.**

Lesson 39

Tone-slap bembe–part 3

Although we didn't analyze the tone-slap bembe rhythm when you first learned it, the open tones in the right hand create a four in that rhythm in six. Now that you've explored the feel of four against six, you should have an easier time with the left-hand patterns in this lesson.

Start by playing four against six on two drums. Play the four in your right hand on the high drum and the six in your left hand on the low drum. If you only have one drum, play the right hand on the side of the drum. All the strokes are open tones, except that the left hand plays a bass tone on the first beat of each measure:

Rhythm 39-1: Four against six

1	2	3	4	5	6	1	2	3	4	5	6
✳		O		O		✳		O		O	
O			O			O			O		

Now leave out the last two open tones in the left hand:

Rhythm 39-2: Four against six (variation)

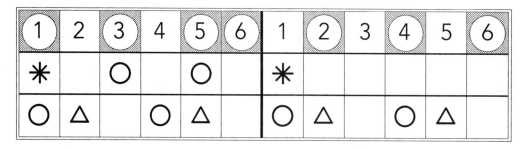

When you get comfortable with this pattern (which sometimes takes a while), just start rocking the right hand forward after the open tones to add slaps:

Rhythm 39-3: Left-hand pattern 7

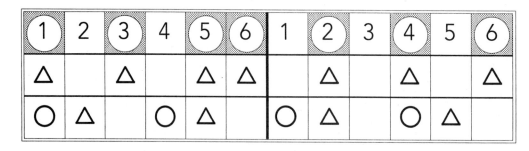

The last two rhythms put the cowbell pattern in six in the left hand against the normal tone-slap pattern in the right. These are tricky, so use all your practice techniques: slow down, break them into pieces, isolate the tough spots and practice them separately, don't grind in mistakes. In the first rhythm, play the cowbell pattern as slaps in the left hand:

Rhythm 39-4: Left-hand pattern 8

In the second rhythm, play the cowbell pattern as open tones in the left hand, except for the two pick-up notes on beat 5 of the first measure and 6 of the second. Play those two as slaps. Concentrate on holding back the right hand while the left hand plays the open tone on beat 6 of the first measure. The hands seem to have a natural urge to play those open tones together:

Rhythm 39-5: Left-hand pattern 9

①	2	③	4	⑤	⑥	1	②	3	④	5	⑥
O		O		△	O		O		O		△
O	△		O	△		O	△		O	△	

We hope these last two difficult rhythms don't have you questioning your competence. Between moments of exultation there will always be many moments when you feel like you're never going to get it right: your timing is off, your hands ache, you can't remember anything, you're going backwards. It's hopeless.

Remember, there can never be peaks without valleys, and there will always be plateaus where progress isn't obvious. But if you love playing and view learning as an end in itself, you can't possibly fail. Be patient with yourself and steady in your practice; the breakthrough will come.

Lesson 40

Tone-slap bembe–part 4

In this lesson, we're going to chart notes that fall on the ANDs between the beats in six. To chart these notes, we've expanded the charts and added a box for the AND after each of the 6 beats. It's as if we put the usual charts under a microscope so we could see the spaces between the boxes.

Before we start putting notes on the ANDs, here's how the tone-slap pattern you already know looks written on one of the new charts. All the notes still fall on numbered beats:

1	+	2	+	3	+	4	+	5	+	6	+
◯		△				◯		△			

As you can see, you're still playing open tones on beats 1 and 4 and slaps on beats 2 and 5; all that's changed is that a box has been added after each numbered beat so that notes on the AND of a beat could be charted.

Now we're going to start using those AND boxes. So far, when you've played four against six, what we've been calling "the six" has actually been two measures of 6 beats each, for a total of 12 beats. The notes of a straight four extended over two measures, falling on beats 1 and 4 of each measure. When the notes of a straight four are charted against a *single* measure of 6 beats they fall on 1, the AND of 2, 4, and the AND of 5. Those are the notes your left hand will be playing in the next rhythm, alternating between tones and slaps. The right plays a straight six, created by adding an extra slap to the normal tone-slap pattern:

Rhythm 40-1: Two-drum bembe with added four

1	+	2	+	3	+	4	+	5	+	6	+
◯			△			◯			△		
◯		△		△		◯		△		△	

Sound familiar? You've already played this rhythm with different techniques before. It's four against six, pure and simple. It's just counted differently.

Now go back to the normal tone-slap pattern in the right hand by taking out the second slap. In the left hand, play only open tones to make the four really stand out:

Rhythm 40-2: Left-hand pattern 10

1	+	2	+	3	+	4	+	5	+	6	+
◯		◯				◯		◯			
◯		△				◯		△			

We didn't chart the bell pattern with this rhythm because it extends over two measures of 6 beats, and this chart is only a single measure long. But you can play the bell pattern with any of these rhythms.

Now you're ready for some serious time travel. In the next rhythm, the left hand plays a straight four, but it doesn't begin on 1. It's shifted over so that the pattern begins on the AND of 1 instead:

Rhythm 40-3: Left-hand pattern 11

1	+	2	+	3	+	4	+	5	+	6	+
	◯			△			◯			△	
◯		△				◯		△			

Because the tones in the left hand fall in between the tone and slap in the right, the combination of those three notes creates an unexpected burst of sound in the rhythm. This left-hand pattern works great as a contrast to a more steady groove, as you'll see in minute.

To make the shifted four stand out so that it cuts through the six, play all open tones in the left hand:

Rhythm 40-4: Left-hand pattern 12

1	+	2	+	3	+	4	+	5	+	6	+
	○		○		○				○		
○	△					○	△				

Now you're ready to try some variations. In the next rhythm, the left hand alternates between a pattern in six you already know and one of the patterns in four you just learned. Because the chart is two measures long, there's room to chart the cowbell pattern:

Rhythm 40-5: Left-hand patterns 4 and 11

1	+	2	+	3	+	4	+	5	+	6	+
				△				○		○	
○		△				○		△			

1	+	2	+	3	+	4	+	5	+	6	+
	○			△				○		△	
○		△				○		△			

To save space in this chart, we've only charted one measure of each left-hand pattern. But feel free to play each pattern for as long as you want before alternating.

Now that your left hand knows how to play both four and six against the steady tone-slap, it can switch from one to the

other in mid-phrase. Like a hawk it can change directions
with precision and speed, darting unexpectedly from the six
to grab a tasty morsel of the four:

Rhythm 40-6: Left-hand pattern 4 (altered)

1	+	2	+	3	+	4	+	5	+	6	+
				△				O		O	
O		△				O		△			

1	+	2	+	3	+	4	+	5	+	6	+
			△					O		O	
O		△				O		△			

We've circled the note grabbed from the four by the left
hand: the slap on the AND of 2 in the second measure.

In the last rhythm, the left hand plays only on ANDs; a tone
on the AND of 1 and a slap on the AND of 2:

Rhythm 40-7: Left-hand pattern 13

1	+	2	+	3	+	4	+	5	+	6	+
	O		△				O		△		
O		△				O		△			

You've built up a large repertoire of variations in the left
hand to play against the tone-slap pattern in the right. Now
put them all together however you want and create your own
compositions. When you're alone, feel free to sample as

much of any variation as you like. Indulge yourself. But when you have company, be sure to serve up generous portions of the basic grooves between spicier variations. Used sparingly, a left-hand pattern in four can add exciting tension to the six. If overused, it will kill the groove and irritate a listener. Don't overspice when you're cooking; always play in good taste.

Lesson 41

The abakwa against four and the cowbell in six

Although it's easy to play the abakwa pattern by itself, because of its unique structure it takes practice and concentration to play it with other rhythms. In this lesson, you're going to play it first against a straight four, then against the tone-slap figure in bembe, and finally against the cowbell pattern in six.

Start by playing the abakwa in your right hand against a straight four in your left. If you have two drums, play the right hand on the high drum and the left hand on the low drum. If you only have one drum, play one hand on the side of the drum and the other on the head:

Rhythm 41-1: The abakwa against four

1	2	3	4	5	6	1	2	3	4	5	6
X			X			X			X		
X	X	X		X	X	X		X	X	X	

**Don't overspice when you're cooking;
always play in good taste.**

Next reverse your hands, and play the straight fours in your
right hand and the abakwa in your left. Play the fours as
open tones on the high drum and the abakwa as bass tones
on the low drum. If you only have one drum, play the
abakwa on the side of the drum with your left hand:

Rhythm 41-2: The abakwa against four

1	2	3	4	5	6	1	2	3	4	5	6
✳	✳	✳		✳	✳	✳		✳	✳	✳	
◯			◯			◯			◯		

Now start rocking your right hand forward and you're
playing the abakwa with the tone-slap bembe:

Rhythm 41-3: Left-hand pattern 14

1	2	3	4	5	6	1	2	3	4	5	6
✳	✳	✳		✳	✳	✳		✳	✳	✳	
◯	△		◯	△		◯	△		◯	△	

Finally, you're going to play the abakwa against the cowbell
pattern in six. This combination, more than any other, will
allow you to feel the full tug of the abakwa against the six.
It's not easy to play. In fact, it's probably the hardest pattern
in this book. So give yourself plenty of time and be patient.
It's worth the effort.

Play the abakwa in your left hand and the bell pattern in
your right. It doesn't matter what hand strokes you use, as
long as you make a different sound with each hand so you
can hear each rhythm distinctly. We broke this combined
rhythm into three 4-beat sections and learned each section
separately before putting them together.

We also spoke out loud what our hands were doing as another way to get the pattern to take hold: "Together-left-together-off . . . ."

Rhythm 41-4: The abakwa against the cowbell in six

1	2	3	4	5	6	1	2	3	4	5	6
X	X	X		X	X	X		X	X	X	
X		X		X	X		X		X		X

We worked on this pattern everywhere: in check-out lines, in waiting rooms, in rush-hour traffic. We figured, why kill time when you can play with it instead? You never know when a rhythm will come together. This is how one of us remembers the moment it happened: Thanksgiving. Uncle Lou's. In the middle of dessert, Aunt Sylvia remembers the radish roses. While she goes back into the kitchen and my relatives groan, the abakwa and cowbell meet secretly beneath the table, dancing in my fingers on the tops of my thighs. Perfect timing. Together at last.

Why kill time when you can play with it instead?

Lesson 42

Implying a six in songo and rumba

There are many ways to combine rhythms in four with rhythms in six. Here's a great one you haven't tried yet: implying a six temporarily within a rhythm in four. The rhythms in four you're going to work with here are songo and the rumba tres golpes, which you already know. Into each of these rhythms, you're going to insert the pattern "ON-off-off-ON-off-off-ON." This pattern kidnaps the listener from the groove in four on a short detour into the land of six. But the detour ends quickly and the four returns in full force, all within a single cycle of the clave.

Here's the pattern in six:

Rhythm 42-1: Six pattern

1	2	3	4	5	6	1	2	3	4	5	6
O	•	✳	O	•	✳	O	•	✳	O	•	✳
L	R	L	R	L	R	L	R	L	R	L	R

Now you're going to take a piece of the pattern in six and insert it into the first measure of songo. The pattern starts on the AND of 1 and ends on the AND of 4. After the pattern ends, watch for the changes at the beginning of the second measure that get the left hand back into position before the slap in the right hand on 2. Play the regular songo three times and insert this variation as the fourth repetition, then repeat the cycle:

Rhythm 42-2: Songo variation

1	+	2	+	3	+	4	+	1	+	2	+	3	+	4	+
	O	•	✳	O	•	✳	O	•	⊖̇	△	•	O	O	◎	◎
	L	R	L	R	L	R	L	R	L	R	L	R	L	R	R

Next you're going to insert the six pattern into the rumba tres golpes. Play the regular part three times and insert this variation as the fourth repetition, then repeat the cycle:

Rhythm 42-3: Rumba tres golpes, variation 1

1	+	2	+	3	+	4	+	1	+	2	+	3	+	4	+
	O	•	✳	O	•	◎	O	O		△	O		△	◎	△
	L	R	L	R	L	R	L	R		L	R		L	R	L

You can also leave off the last open tone of the six pattern and return to the rumba one eighth-note beat earlier. To do this, play a slap in the left hand on the AND of 4 in the first measure instead of an open tone:

Rhythm 42-4: Rumba tres golpes, variation 2

①	+	2	⊕	3	+	4	⊕	1	+	②	+	③	+	4	+
	○	•	✳	○	•	◎	△	○		△	○		△	◎	△
	L	R	L	R	L	R	L	R		L	R		L	R	L

Now play the regular rumba and insert one of these two variations every four repetitions.

Lesson 43

Cycles of four against cycles of six

In this last lesson, you're going to play two rhythms of unequal length at the same time. This means that they'll start together but won't come together again until at least one of the rhythms has gone through more than one repetition or cycle.

For example, when one rhythm is 8 beats long and the other is 6 beats long, if they start at the same time, they won't come together again until 24 beats later. By then, the 8-beat rhythm will have gone through 3 cycles and the 6-beat rhythm will have gone through 4, for a combined cycle of 24 beats.

Because there are two drum parts to the rhythms in this lesson, it would help to have a partner to play with. Each rhythm is easy to play by itself. Woven together, each pair creates a wonderfully intricate braid of sound. If you don't have a partner, the recording that comes with this book has an extended version of each rhythm played separately, so you can play along.

Each pair of rhythms you're going to play in this lesson is made up of one rhythm in six and one in four. Earlier you played the four inside the six, where the length of each rhythm was the same; the four and the six started and ended together. Here the length of each rhythm is different, which means they won't start and end together on every repetition.

In the first pair, the rhythm in six is the first bembe rhythm you learned: tumbao in six. Counting each eighth note as a beat, it's 6 beats long:

Rhythm 7-1: Tumbao in six

1	2	3	4	5	6
▽	•	△	•	○	○
L	L	R	L	R	R

The rhythm in four in the first pair is the first half of the calypso middle drum part. Counting each eighth note as a beat, it's 8 beats long:

Rhythm 1-2: Calypso middle drum part (1st half)

1	+	2	+	3	+	4	+
○	•	•	○	○	•	•	•
R	L	R	L	R	L	R	L

In the next chart, tumbao in six is written above calypso. Play one rhythm while your partner plays the other. Remember to keep going after you reach the end of the first row. Start together and keep the eighth notes the same length in both rhythms. After you start, you won't come together again until 24 beats later, when you start the chart over:

Rhythm 43-1: Tumbao in six and calypso

1	2	3	4	5	6	1	2	3	4	5	6
⊽	•	△	•	◯	◯	⊽	•	△	•	◯	◯
L	L	R	L	R	R	L	L	R	L	R	R

1	+	2	+	3	+	4	+	1	+	2	+
◯	•	•	◯	◯	•	•	•	◯	•	•	◯
R	L	R	L	R	L	R	L	R	L	R	L

1	2	3	4	5	6	1	2	3	4	5	6
⊽	•	△	•	◯	◯	⊽	•	△	•	◯	◯
L	L	R	L	R	R	L	L	R	L	R	R

3	+	4	+	1	+	2	+	3	+	4	+
◯	•	•	•	◯	•	•	◯	◯	•	•	•
R	L	R	L	R	L	R	L	R	L	R	L

Now you're going to combine two more rhythms with
unequal cycles and play them together. The rhythm in six is
longer than the last one; it has 24 beats in its cycle:

Rhythm 43-2: Rhythm in six, high drum

1	2	3	4	5	6	1	2	3	4	5	6
✳	△	△	✳	△		✳	△	△	✳	△	
L	R	L	R	L		L	R	L	R	L	

1	2	3	4	5	6	1	2	3	4	5	6
✳	△	△	✳	△	△	△	△	△	✳	△	
L	R	L	R	L	R	L	R	L	R	L	

The rhythm in four is one of the drum parts in bomba; it has
8 beats in its cycle:

Rhythm 22-1: Bomba middle drum part

1	+	2	+	3	+	4	+	1	+	2	+	3	+	4	+
✳	●	●	△	✳	○	○	●	✳	●	●	△	✳	○	○	●
R	L	R	L	R	L	R	L	R	L	R	L	R	L	R	L

Here are the two rhythms together. The rhythm in six is
written on top. The combined cycle is 24 beats long:

Rhythm 43-3: Rhythm in six and bomba

1	2	3	4	5	6	1	2	3	4	5	6
✳	△	△	✳	△		✳	△	△	✳	△	
L	R	L	R	L		L	R	L	R	L	

1	+	2	+	3	+	4	+	1	+	2	+
✳	•	•	△	✳	•	○	○	✳	•	•	△
R	L	R	L	R	L	R	L	R	L	R	L

1	2	3	4	5	6	1	2	3	4	5	6
✳	△	△	✳	△	△	△	△	△	✳	△	
L	R	L	R	L	R	L	R	L	R	L	

3	+	4	+	1	+	2	+	3	+	4	+
✳	•	○	○	✳	•	•	△	✳	•	○	○
R	L	R	L	R	L	R	L	R	L	R	L

One afternoon, just for fun, we decided to put these two rhythms together to see how they'd sound. It wasn't long before the pleasure got so intense we had to stop. Our bodies could not contain the excitement and continue playing at the same time. The constant shifting of the weave of the two rhythms kept us deliciously off balance on a musical Tilt-A-Whirl. You can experiment by playing this rhythm in six with other rhythms in four. Try it with calypso and tumbao. With just about anything in four it cooks.

Well, we've taken you as far as we can right now. We hope we've made this stretch of the journey a little easier than it otherwise might have been. But don't stop now. The path goes on forever. Keep the beat going. If you haven't already, go out and find a teacher who can take you further. Teach what you know to someone else. Spread the word. Make the world a funkier place.

Keep the beat going.
Make the world a funkier place.

12

Sources for further study

Amira, John and Steven Cornelius, *The Music of Santeria: Traditional Rhythms of the Bata Drums*, White Cliffs Media Co., 1992.

Flatischler, Reinhard, *The Forgotten Power of Rhythm: Ta Ke Ti Na*, Liferhythm, 1992.

Gerard, Charley with Marty Sheller, *Salsa: The Rhythm of Latin Music*, White Cliffs Media Co., 1989.

Hart, Mickey with Jay Stevens, *Drumming at the Edge of Magic: A Journey into the Spirit of Percussion*, Harper San Francisco, 1990.

Malabe, Frank and Bob Weiner, *Afro-Cuban Rhythms for Drumset*, Manhattan Music Publications, 1990.

Mauleon, Rebeca, *Salsa Guidebook For Piano and Ensemble*, Sher Music Co., 1993.

Roberts, John Storm, *Black Music of Two Worlds*, Morrow Paperbacks, 1974.

Roberts, John Storm, *The Latin Tinge: The Impact of Latin American Music on the United States*, Original Music, 1985.

Sulsbruck, Berger, *Latin-American Percussion: Rhythms and rhythm instruments from Cuba and Brazil*, Den Rytmiske Aftenskoles Forlag, 1986.

Wilcken, Lois featuring Frisner Augustin, *The Drums of Vodou*, White Cliffs Media Co., 1992.

13

Index of rhythms

Also available from Dancing Hands Music

Conga Drumming— A Beginner's Video Guide

"**The perfect addition to the book**"—LATIN BEAT

$29.95

This video shows how to play the basic parts for all the rhythms in the book CONGA DRUMMING. It features Jorge Bermudez, who puts special emphasis on proper playing technique. Special guest Raul Rekow of Santana solos on congas and bongos in the ensemble performances and electrifying Cuban dancer Rosie Lopez Morè—from the legendary Tropicana nightclub in Havana—dances the rumba.

"**Slammin! The best video for learning to play congas**"—CHALO EDUARDO, PERCUSSIONIST WITH SERGIO MENDES.

"**Few videos capture the spirit** of fun as well as CONGA DRUMMING. All the basics are covered and the educational information is interspersed with burning performances by the ensemble. When Rosie Lopez Morè is on screen the video is ablaze with energy. While there is much to be learned from CONGA DRUMMING, it also provides a highly entertaining viewing experience that will inspire any beginning conga drummer."—DRUM MAGAZINE

Conga Drumming Practice Partner CD

If you don't have a drum machine, this is the next best thing. It contains extended recordings of the son clave, rumba clave, and 6/8 cowbell (played slow, medium, and fast) to play along with while you practice. **$9.95**

A Rhythmic Vocabulary— A Musician's Guide to Understanding and Improvising with Rhythm

$29.95

This new 208-page book by Alan Dworsky and Betsy Sansby is a step-by-step, comprehensive course in rhythm for any musician. It presents hundreds of traditional African and Afro-Cuban hand drum patterns organized according to their structure and explains how to vary and combine the patterns when you improvise or solo. It comes with a practice CD containing extended recordings of the son clave and 6/8 cowbell at seven different speeds each.

Jaguar at Half Moon Lake
A new CD of original music by Dancing Hands

$13.95

"**Only a barbarous savage could resist these gorgeous melodies and mesmerizing rhythms.**"—DIRTY LINEN

JAGUAR is a synthesis of world beat, funk, and folk music featuring Indie-award winning Dean Magraw on acoustic guitar and Alan Dworsky on conga drums. The rhythm section also features several world percussionists, including Congolese Master Drummer, Coster Massamba on djembe, Jorge Bermudez on bongos and timbales, and Marc Anderson on frame drum, talking drum, clay pot, and shakers.

We also carry lots of instructional books and videos on hand drumming and hard-to-find CDs of great drumming from around the world. Call for a catalog, or check out our website at www.dancinghands.com.

To order by mail, send a check or money order to **Dancing Hands Music**, 4275 Churchill Circle, Minnetonka, MN 55345. From outside the U.S., the phone and fax number is 612-933-0781. Shipping is only $3.00 no matter what you order.

Call toll-free to order with your VISA or MasterCard: **1-800-898-8036**